IMPROVING
LEADERSHIP EFFECTIVENESS:
THE LEADER MATCH CONCEPT

IMPROVING LEADERSHIP EFFECTIVENESS:
THE LEADER MATCH CONCEPT

FRED E. FIEDLER
MARTIN M. CHEMERS
with
LINDA MAHAR

John Wiley & Sons, Inc.
New York • London • Sydney • Toronto

Editors: Judy Wilson and Irene Brownstone
Production Manager: Ken Burke
Cartoons: Martha Weston

Library of Congress Cataloging in Publication Data

Fiedler, Fred Edward.
        Improving leadership effectiveness.

        (A Wiley self-teaching guide)
        Bibliography: p. 215
        Includes index.
        1. Leadership—Programmed instruction. 2. Super-
vision of employees—Programmed instruction. I. Chemers,
Martin M., joint author. II. Title.
HM141.F46   301.15'53'077   76-20632
ISBN 0-471-25811-3

Printed in the United States of America

76   77   10   9 8 7 6 5 4 3 2 1

Contents

Acknowledgments

The research program on which this training manual is based was begun in 1951 and represents the effort of many co-workers who were at one time or another associated with the Group Effectiveness Research Laboratory at the University of Illinois and the Organizational Research Group at the University of Washington in Seattle. It is a privilege to express our appreciation to all of them. We are especially indebted to our colleagues, Drs. Paul M. Bons, Louis S. Csoka, L. David Jacobs, Gary Latham, Bill Curtis, and M. Peter Scontrino for their many thoughtful comments and suggestions.

The development of the Leader Match training program is founded on research support from various military and civilian agencies and on the encouragement and assistance which we received from key officials in these agencies. We wish to express our heartfelt thanks to: the Office of Naval Research and to Drs. John Nagay and Bert King of the Organizational Effectiveness Research Program; the Advanced Research Projects Agency and Drs. Robert A. Young and George Lawrence of the Human Resources Research Division; the Office of the Chief of Naval Education and Training and in particular to Captain Bruce Stone, Captain (CH) Carl Auel, and Drs. William Haythorn and Ralph Chandler; the Army Research Institute for the Behavioral Sciences and its director, Dr. J.E. Uhlaner; Los Amigos de las Americas and the Rev. Guy Bevil, the Rev. Dr. T.J. Grosser, and Bob Black; King County (Washington) Executive John B. Spellman and department directors Charles Collins, Jean DeSpain, Jack Lynch, Thomas Ryan, and Lawrence Waldt. This Self-Teaching Guide version for business, industry, and volunteer organizations was made possible through the encouragement and financial support of John Wiley & Sons, Inc. and Wiley editors Judy V. Wilson and Irene F. Brownstone.

Finally, our thanks to our respective spouses, Judith Fiedler, Arlene Chemers, and Dennis Mahar not only for the moral support which they so freely *had* to give, but for sharing with us as professional colleagues their expertise and their talents.

Foreword

One of the most difficult personnel decisions in management is what sort of person to promote into a leadership position. The familiar cliche that what individuals have done in the past is the best indication of what they will do in the future is almost useless because there are no data on previously demonstrated managerial capabilities. True, there may be information on community projects and similar off-the-job situations, but translation is difficult and at times irrelevant. As a result, selections are frequently made on the basis of excellence in former, different assignments. The best engineer may thus become a supervisor or the best toolmaker a foreman. While technical capability is certainly desirable and even critical, we have learned to our sorrow that it is not enough for successful leadership which places a premium on interpersonal skills.

The 1940s and 1950s saw a serious attempt to use personality tests to identify the human qualities most likely to be associated with managerial success. Personality inventories, self-ratings, and interest checklists were widely administered. The early ones were generally straightforward, simple to take and score. As it became apparent that intelligent people could adjust their results to project their perception of the desired personality, more and more complex instruments were developed to obscure the meaning of responses. Gestalt techniques such as the Rorschach inkblot test and the Thematic Apperception Test were tried. For these instruments the skill and judgment of the interpreter were critical and their cost discouraged wide usage. The more fundamental problem, however, was that all these devices assumed that personality characteristics could be measured and that some were "good" and others "poor" for leadership purposes. For the most part, correlation of success with the results of such tests proved to be so low that their value was questionable. Moreover, present Equal Opportunity regulations severely limit their use.

The next wave of research was focused on defining successful managerial style. Much was learned about the impact of style on subordinate performance. Most researchers seemed, however, to be seeking a single "right" or "appropriate" style (although psychologists probably would not admit it). Undoubtedly influenced heavily by McGregor's Theory Y of management, many managers in the Fifties and Sixties engaged in workshops, self-analysis, and group exercises in an attempt to analyze their style and modify it to become more "democratic." Some success can be claimed for this effort, although much reported improvement in interpersonal sensitivity was on the home front, rather than at work. In business or industry, lack of reinforcement from superiors or associates was often given as the reason for failure to implement good resolutions. In any event, the impact can best be described as mixed.

Throughout this period Fred Fiedler conducted his research. He looked not only at individuals and how they behaved, but also at the kind of situation in which they were functioning well or badly. Because of this dual focus on person and situation, the desirability of more than one leadership style to accommodate a variety of situations became clear. To those of us working in the selection field it provided a blinding flash of insight. His research matched our experience! All of us had seen at least one highly successful individual fail when moved to another position which required the same or similiar technical strength. And, of course, all of us had observed a wide variety of successful styles among members of management. What Fred Fiedler's work did was to make it possible for people to focus on understanding and accepting their own style and recognizing its positive and negative effects, rather than trying to change their style. As a personal strategy this surely offered considerable promise.

There was just one problem. With all the good intentions in the world, it was very difficult to get a reliable reading on one's style or, if one were obtained, to know how to evaluate situational factors.

This Self-Teaching Guide, *Improving Leadership Effectiveness*, helps resolve the dilemma. Fiedler and his associates not only supply a quick understanding of the philosophy and underlying theory of leadership (with appropriate disclaimers of miracles), but also provide a straightforward, non-threatening way for a person to rate himself or herself on a number of style factors. They then supply a series of rating scales for evaluating situational characteristics so that appropriate matches can be made between the two. The concept has already made a distinctive contribution to management *thinking*. The devices proposed for rating and comparative purposes may also make a unique contribution to management *action*.

This book is of interest and help to individual workers who are considering a leadership position. It is equally useful to personnel placement and organizational development specialists concerned with recommending qualified candidates for open positions. It is valuable to persons already in a supervisory or managerial position who should feel continuing concern about leadership capability, both their own and that of their subordinates. Of special interest to executives is Part IV "Management of Managers." Here are suggested ways of analyzing the styles of subordinate managers to determine the kinds of working situations that are likely to help them achieve success. It sheds light on that difficult top management concern: "How can I influence the results achieved by managers in my organization without interfering with their own methods and practices?"

If I seem enthusiastic about this book, it is because I believe it fills a great need and will be useful to a large number of present and aspiring leaders and their mentors.

June, 1976

Marion S. Kellogg
Vice President,
General Electric Company

PART I
Identifying Your Leadership Style

CHAPTER ONE

Introduction to Leader Match

The quality of leadership, more than any other single factor, determines the success or failure of an organization. This is as true of national affairs as it is of a small work crew. Without George Washington's skill and determination, the Revolutionary War might have had a different outcome. Without the leadership of Abraham Lincoln, the Union might have been destroyed. And men like Henry Ford, Thomas Edison, and J.P. Morgan left an indelible imprint on American business and industry, just as Susan B. Anthony and Martin Luther King, Jr. helped to change the social roles of large groups of Americans.

Leadership is an extremely complex interpersonal relationship. If there is no follower, there can be no leader. Members of a group implicitly or explicitly let one person, the leader, make certain decisions and judgments in order to accomplish the group's task. Leadership can only be exercised in groups in which people want to accomplish a common goal. The effectiveness of the leader depends, therefore, not only on him but also on those he leads, and the conditions under which he must operate.

Leadership has different meanings to different people. It includes the ability to counsel, to manage conflict, to inspire loyalty, and to imbue subordinates with the desire to remain on the job. It also means the effective accomplishment of the primary task: the performance of a job for which a work unit or an organization has been established. We shall here deal primarily with this task-performance focus of leadership. This does not mean that other duties of the leader are unimportant or uninteresting. These are, however, currently addressed in many human relations workshops and training programs. This manual is devoted primarily to the problem of how to lead effectively, an important problem for the manager in business, industry, or government, as well as for the military leader. As you begin this leadership training program, some of the following questions have probably come to your mind.

What will the program do for me? This self-instructional program is designed to help you become a more effective leader. It is based on the well established notion that most people are effective in some leadership situations and ineffective in others. It is difficult to visualize a brilliant but crusty military commander like General Patton as an effective leader of a sensitivity group, or as the director of a research laboratory. It is equally unlikely that the famous movie producer, Samuel Goldwyn, would have made a very effective manager of a bookkeeping department.

We cannot expect ourselves to be outstanding in all jobs and situations. This manual will help you to recognize the particular leadership situations in which you are most likely to succeed, and it will suggest ways of dealing with situations in which you are apt to be ineffective. Obviously, if you know how to avoid situations in which you are likely to fail, you greatly increase your chances for success.

What is new about this approach?   This training program is based on a theory of leadership called the "Contingency Model," which has been developed over the past 25 years. This theory holds that the effectiveness of a group or an organization depends on two interacting or "contingent" factors. The first is the personality of the leaders which determine their leadership style. The second factor is the amount of control and influence which the situation provides leaders over their group's behavior, the task, and the outcome. This factor is called "situational control." (Those familiar with the Contingency Model will recall this as "situational favorableness," a term which was confusing to some people.)

Is this a new theory?   Not at all. More than 200 journal articles, books, and reports have been written about the Contingency Model, and most standard textbooks in the field of organization theory and management, or social psychology, devote space to it. It is one of the most researched and best validated leadership theories at this time.

This training program is designed as a *practical* guide to better leadership. We shall discuss theoretical issues only when absolutely essential. However, you must understand the basic principles in order to apply them properly to your particular leadership situation. You will not be able to apply rules blindly and unthinkingly. Leadership is an art which requires sound judgment.

How well does this program work?   A number of studies have been conducted in different types of organizations, e.g., in a volunteer public health organization, among supervisors and middle managers of a government agency, among police sergeants, and in various military units. Leaders trained with this manual reported that they could apply the principles of this training program and that they found it helpful in dealing with their leadership jobs. Most importantly, in each of these studies, conducted under controlled conditions, randomly selected, trained leaders performed significantly and substantially better than did the comparable groups of untrained leaders.

What does this program require of you?   You will need to read carefully the discussion sections which explain the principles on which this training is based and you will need to test your knowledge by completing the various exercises and quizzes in the program. The general procedure which the manual will follow is described below.

ORGANIZATION OF THE MANUAL

The manual is divided into four major parts. Part I is concerned with identifying your leadership style. Part II will provide you with the tools for accurately diagnosing and classifying leadership situations. This part is the longest and consists of five chapters. It will show you how to measure your leadership situation and how to assess, within broad limits, the leadership situations of those who work with you.

Part III will discuss how to match your leadership style with your situation and how to change your leadership situation, if necessary, to obtain maximum effectiveness. Part IV is directed to leaders of subordinate leaders. It discusses how to provide subordinate leaders with situation in which they can perform most effectively. If you are now in a leadership position which does not require the supervision of other leaders, you may choose to skip this section or save it for a later time.

Throughout this training program we shall assume that the leader is technically qualified to perform his job. No matter how appropriate his leadership style may be, you would not want the chief of your brain surgery team to be without medical training nor the captain of an airplane to be without a pilot's license.

How do you proceed?   Each chapter begins with a brief discussion of the principles you must know in order to apply the leadership theory on which this program is based. Each will be followed by exercises called "probes" which let you evaluate how well you have understood the material in the chapter.

Each probe typically consists of a short case study or an incident which presents a problem in leadership and illustrates the main points of the chapter. Choose the best of several alternative explanations or decisions for the problem.

Indicate your first choice by writing a "1" next to the answer you consider the best. Then turn to the following page for the "feedback" which tells whether or not you made the right choice and discusses the answer. If your answer was correct, you will be instructed to turn to the next probe or to the following chapter.

If you did not choose the best answer, the feedback page will direct you to reread the section of the chapter which you may have misunderstood. You should then try to answer the question again. Mark this second answer "2" and mark "3" in case you have to make a third try. Many people find it useful to read through all the feedback pages which go with each probe since the explanations for the incorrect answers are often helpful to better understand the material.

We suggest that you keep a bookmark or slip of paper handy to mark your place while you check your answers and review appropriate material.

Each chapter is followed by a short summary which will help you review the material after you have taken a break in your study. These review sections cover the new terms in the training program, and the section Self-

Tests will indicate whether you are ready to continue to the next part of the program. The program concludes with a bibliography of suggested readings which may interest readers of a more theoretical bent.

How long will it take? This depends on your reading speed and on how much you already know. The average time for completion of the training is about five hours, some take as long as eight hours and a few have finished in four. This also is a matter of personal preference. Some people like to linger over the material while others like to work under pressure.

It is advisable to space your study of this material over at least two or three days. The best breaking points are at the conclusion of each chapter. *Do not skip over chapters.* In order to derive maximum benefit from this program, you must work through successive chapters in sequence with appropriate breaks.

CHAPTER TWO

Identifying Your Leadership Style

As you will recall from Chapter One, your performance as a leader depends primarily on the match between your personality and the degree to which you have control over your leadership situation. This chapter will help you identify your underlying goals in the leadership situation. These determine how you will relate to the people who work for you, and under what conditions your particular leadership style will be most effective. *To do this, it is essential that you carefully read the following instructions and complete the Least Preferred Co-worker (LPC) Scale on page 8.*

INSTRUCTIONS

Throughout your life you will have worked in many groups with a wide variety of different people — on your job, in social groups, in church organizations, in volunteer groups, on athletic teams, and in many other situations. Some of your co-workers may have been very easy to work with in attaining the group's goals, while others were less so.

Think of all the people with whom you have ever worked, and then think of the person with whom you could work *least well*. He or she may be someone with whom you work now or with whom you have worked in the past. This does not have to be the person you liked least well, but should be the person with whom you had the most difficulty getting a job done, the *one* individual with whom you could work *least well*.

Describe this person on the scale which follows by placing an "X" in the appropriate space. The scale consists of pairs of words which are opposite in meaning, such as *Very Neat* and *Very Untidy*. Between each pair of words are eight spaces to form a scale like this:

Very Neat ___ ___ ___ ___ ___ ___ ___ ___ Very Untidy
8   7   6   5   4   3   2   1

Thus, if your ordinarily think of the person with whom you work least well as being *quite neat*, you would mark an "X" in the space marked 7, like this:

Very Neat	**X**							Very Untidy
8	7	6	5	4	3	2	1	
Very Neat	Quite Neat	Somewhat Neat	Slightly Neat	Slightly Untidy	Somewhat Untidy	Quite Untidy	Very Untidy	

If you ordinarily think of this person as being only *slightly neat,* you would put your "X" in space 5. If you would think of this person as being *very untidy* (not neat), you would put your "X" in space 1.

Look at the words at both ends of the line before you mark your "X". *There are no right or wrong answers.* Work rapidly; your first answer is likely to be the best. Do not omit any items, and mark each item only once.

Now go to the next page and describe the person with whom you can work least well.

Think of the person with whom you can work least well . . .

LEAST PREFERRED CO-WORKER (LPC) SCALE

Scoring

Pleasant	8	7	6	5	4	3	2	1	Unpleasant	3
Friendly	8	7	6	5	4	3	2	1	Unfriendly	7 10
Rejecting	1	2	3	4	5	6	7	8	Accepting	3
Tense	1	2	3	4	5	6	7	8	Relaxed	5 18
Distant	1	2	3	4	5	6	7	8	Close	4
Cold	1	2	3	4	5	6	7	8	Warm	6 28
Supportive	8	7	6	5	4	3	2	1	Hostile	3
Boring	1	2	3	4	5	6	7	8	Interesting	5
Quarrelsome	1	2	3	4	5	6	7	8	Harmonious	2 38
Gloomy	1	2	3	4	5	6	7	8	Cheerful	4
Open	8	7	6	5	4	3	2	1	Guarded	6 48
Backbiting	1	2	3	4	5	6	7	8	Loyal	2 50
Untrustworthy	1	2	3	4	5	6	7	8	Trustworthy	3
Considerate	8	7	6	5	4	3	2	1	Inconsiderate	3
Nasty	1	2	3	4	5	6	7	8	Nice	3 59
Agreeable	8	7	6	5	4	3	2	1	Disagreeable	3
Insincere	1	2	3	4	5	6	7	8	Sincere	2 64
Kind	8	7	6	5	4	3	2	1	Unkind	3 67

Total 67

Your score on the LPC scale is a measure of your leadership style. More specifically, it indicates your primary motivation or goal in a work setting. Although there may be several people with whom you cannot work well, the person whom you should have described is the *one* person with whom you *least* prefer working.

To determine your LPC score, turn back to this scale and place the numbers you checked in the column at the right of the page. Add your responses, and enter the total at the bottom of the page. *Be sure to check your addition!*

We use certain scores to identify two types of leadership styles.

- If your score is 64 or above, you are a *high LPC* person. We call high LPC people *relationship-motivated*.

- If your score is 57 or below, you are a *low LPC* person. We call low LPC people *task-motivated*.

There is, of course, a group in the middle which falls between those who are clearly relationship-motivated and those who are clearly task-motivated. It is difficult to draw a personality sketch for this middle group. First of all, a person who falls somewhat above a score of 60 at one time might fall somewhat below it at another time and vice versa. Second, some people in this middle group may belong to a category of people with a mix of motivations and goals. If your score falls between 58 and 63, you will need to determine for yourself into which of these groups you belong.

The way the LPC scale works is fairly simple. The individual who describes his least preferred co-worker in very negative, rejecting terms (low LPC) essentially says, "Work is extremely important to me; therefore, if you are a poor co-worker and prevent me in my efforts to get the job done, then I cannot accept you in any other respects either." Therefore, he describes his LPC as unfriendly, uncooperative, hostile, etc. This is a strong emotional reaction to people with whom the leader cannot work, who frustrate him in getting a job done. This type of leader is called a *task-motivated* person.

The high LPC leader basically says, "Even if I can't work with you, you may still be relatively pleasant, industrious, or sincere." In other words, the relationship with others is sufficiently important, compared to the task, that the individual can clearly differentiate between his negative reactions to someone who is a poor co-worker and his appreciation of this person as an individual. This type of leader is called a *relationship-motivated* person.

It is important to realize that both types of leaders are very effective in situations which match their style and that neither tends to be outstanding in all situations. We cannot stress this point too often. Both leadership styles have some good points and some less desirable characteristics, and each can be equally effective in situations which fit their style.

The rest of this chapter will give you more specific descriptions of the behavioral tendencies of individuals who score high and low on the LPC scale. You will, of course, want to see how well these descriptions fit you. Don't expect to find each and every attribute of the high or the low LPC person in yourself or in others whose LPC score you happen to know. These sketches are "types." They are designed to give you a realistic feeling for the average person who scores high or low on the LPC scale.

It is sometimes very difficult for individuals to recognize themselves in these descriptions. People behave quite differently under various conditions, and often you may not behave as you think you do. Most of us are quite startled when we accidentally hear how others describe us: "Is this really me?" or "Is this actually the way I behaved that time?" These are not uncommon reactions to hearing how we appeared to others on various occasions. It is similar to the way people react when they see themselves on TV or when they hear themselves on a tape recorder. Nevertheless, the LPC scale *tends* to give an accurate reflection of a leader's personality in various situations.

As we said before, each leadership style has advantages and disadvantages. Nobody is perfect, and the secret of effective leadership is to clearly recognize your strengths as well as your weaknesses. You may not like everything about your leadership style, and everything that describes your type may not fit you as a person. These descriptions are *guidelines* which will help you improve your leadership performance.

RELATIONSHIP-MOTIVATED LEADERS (LPC score of 64 and above)

Although high LPC leaders are concerned with doing a good job, their primary motivation or goal is to have good interpersonal relations with others. Their self-esteem depends to a large extent on how other people relate to them. They are therefore likely to pay particular attention to their group members, and be concerned about their feelings. When they find themselves in stressful or anxiety-arousing situations, they seek the support of their group and are eager to maintain good group morale. They are able to see different viewpoints, and tend to deal effectively with complex problems which require creative and resourceful thinking.

In the work group, relationship-motivated leaders encourage different ideas and the participation of group members. They are tolerant of complexity and ambiguity and sensitive to the needs and feelings of their subordinates. Consequently, they are able to minimize interpersonal conflict.

In low control situations, i.e. more stressful or challenging situations, this behavior frequently becomes exaggerated, often to the extent that the individual does not perform very well in fulfilling task requirements. High LPC leaders often become so involved in discussions and consultations with subordinates that they fail to pay sufficient attention to the job. Support from their group becomes overly important. Consequently, they become reluctant to alienate or anger them.

In moderate control situations, relationship-motivated leaders are at their best. They are appropriately concerned with interpersonal relations and able to deal with them effectively. Their sensitivity to interpersonal problems allows them to cope with difficult subordinates; and their creative ability and imagination are challenged by tasks which require them to innovate.

In high control situations, that is, when relationship-motivated leaders no longer need to worry about relations with their group, they may become more concerned with how they appear to their boss and to others outside their immediate work group. Because they want to make a good impression, they may plow ahead with their task, appearing to be less considerate of the feelings of their subordinates. Although they still want approval from their employees, favorably impressing their boss or outsiders often becomes more important. Under these conditions the high LPC leaders often tend to behave in an autocratic manner by structuring the work situation and the task.

When the situation becomes too relaxed and does not require the establishment of guidelines or the generation of ideas, high LPC leaders are no longer challenged; they may lose interest, and appear bored and aloof to their group members.

Summary of High LPC Leaders

Relationship-motivated, or high LPC leaders (score of 64 or above), tend to accomplish the task through good interpersonal relations with the group in situations in which the group as a whole participates in the task performance. When their primary goal has been accomplished and things are under control, they may behave in a brusque, authoritarian manner which is seen as inconsiderate by subordinates. In a tense, anxiety-arousing situation, they may become so concerned with interpersonal relationships that they fail to accomplish the task.

TASK-MOTIVATED LEADERS (LPC score of 57 and below)

Task-motivated individuals need to get things done. They gain self-esteem from tangible, measurable evidence of performance and achievement. They are strongly motivated to accomplish successfully any task to which they have committed themselves, even if there are no external rewards.

In challenging situations in which their control is low, they feel most comfortable working from clear guidelines and standard operating procedures. When these are missing from a job, they try to discover or develop such guidelines. In this situation they perform very well. They are no-nonsense persons who are apt to take charge early — in committee meetings they tend to move right in and arrange available materials and be impatient to get down to business. They quickly assign tasks, provide schedules, and monitor productivity. They are concerned about achieving task success through clear and standardized work procedures. At times, when subordinates wish to discuss the situation, their impatience to get the job done may irritate their group members. In this situation they are generally not very concerned or oriented toward interpersonal problems and generally are not too attuned to interpersonal conflict.

In situations in which they are in complete control, and don't have to worry as much about getting the job done, they tend to be considerate and pleasant. Under these conditions they are able to relax and assume an easygoing manner, content to let their group handle the job. By the same token, they resent interference from others who are above them in authority.

In situations of moderate control, and especially situations involving interpersonal conflict, task-motivated leaders tend to feel out of their element. They become engrossed in the task and pay little or no attention to the needs and feelings of group members, and ignore imminent conflicts within the goup, with the result that their performance tends to be poorer.

Low LPC leaders differ from high LPC leaders in being able to perform relatively well under stressful conditions or those in which they have relatively little control. They also tend to perform well in situations in which they have a great deal of control. Low LPC people are *as well liked* as the high LPC leaders even though they place task accomplishment above interpersonal relations. A low LPC score does not necessarily mean having poor or unpleasant interpersonal relations. On the contrary, many low LPC leaders get along extremely well with their subordinates.

Summary of Low LPC Leaders

Task-motivated, or low LPC leaders (score of 57 and below), are strongly motivated to accomplish successfully any task to which they have committed themselves. They do this through clear and standardized work procedures and a no-nonsense attitude about getting down to work. Although they want to get the job done, they will care about the opinions and feelings of subordinates as long as everything is under control. But in low control situations, they will tend to neglect the feelings of group members in an effort to get the job done — "business before pleasure!" For them there is no conflict between the esteem they get from subordinates and the esteem from their boss. They use the group to do the job, and when they feel that the situation is under control, they try to do this as pleasantly as possible.

Remember that the descriptions of relationship- and task-motivated persons are useful and fit many people quite well. However, you should always keep one important point in mind: Whether you are a "true type" or a combination of leadership types, *your effectiveness as a manager will depend on how well your individual personality and leadership style fit the requirements of your leadership situation*, and not whether you scored high or low on the LPC scale.

Now try the probes on the following pages to see how well you have understood the discussion of leadership style. Remember to mark your first choice with a "1" and subsequent choices with a "2" or "3" if necessary. Then turn to the following page to obtain feedback on whether you made the correct selection.

⟶ **PROBE 1**

You have just finished reading about the types of leadership motivations measured by the Least Preferred Co-Worker Scale. Which of the following descriptions most accurately captures the meaning of LPC?

_____ (a) A measure which predicts that an individual will behave in one particular way in almost *every* leadership situation.

_____ (b) Behavior which changes constantly from situation to situation with little consistency or predictability.

_____ (c) A set of needs and values which determine what a leader will see as most important in various leadership situations.

Go to the next page for feedback.

FEEDBACK ←——————————————————————

(a) **You chose (a):** *A measure which predicts that an individual will be-have in one particular way in almost* every *leadership situation.* This is not correct. While the LPC score predicts an individual's motivation, that is, his or her major goals and values as they relate to leadership, the LPC score does not show that an individual will behave the same in every situation. Remember that relationship-motivated (high LPC) leaders are very consider-ate of subordinates when they are not in control of the situation; when they are in complete control, they may act in an inconsiderate, distant manner. Likewise, task-motivated (low LPC) leaders are sometimes relaxed and easy-going when they are in complete control of the situation, but when the leader-ship situation is low in control, they tend to become concerned with the task and to neglect interpersonal relationships.

Put a bookmark at Probe 1 to hold your place. Then reread Chapter Two and try Probe 1 again.

(b) **You chose (b):** *Behavior which changes constantly from situation to situation with little consistency or predictability.* Incorrect. If the leader's behavior is so changeable and unpredictable, there would be little purpose in measuring it and relating it to other aspects of the leadership situ-ation. Under these conditions we could not use LPC as a measure of person-ality which will affect group or organizational performance.

Put a bookmark at Probe 1 to hold your place. Then reread Chapter Two and try Probe 1 again.

(c) **You chose (c):** *A set of needs and values which determine what a leader will see as most important in various leadership situations.* This choice is correct. While we cannot predict a single individual's behavior with unerring accuracy, the LPC score gives us a general idea of a leader's needs and motivation. Different types of leaders not only seek somewhat different things in leadership situations, they also perceive and react to these situations differently. The LPC measure allows us to predict the general motivation of different leaders as an important step in matching leaders and situations for maximum effectiveness.

Now try Probe 2 on the next page. You're doing fine!

--➤ **PROBE 2**

The foreman who works for you has just taken the LPC scale and tells you that this measure can't be any good. He has a high LPC score and is, therefore, supposed to be concerned with interpersonal relations. However, he doesn't get along with everybody and he is certainly concerned with the task because he works hard. *What would you say?*

___/___ (a) The foreman does not understand the nature of the LPC score. He assumes that a high LPC person will always behave in the same way, and therefore, that LPC can't be any good.

_____ (b) The foreman's score is probably in error since he works hard and is concerned with the task. This suggests that he is more likely to be low LPC.

_____ (c) The foreman probably misunderstood the scoring system. A person with a high LPC score is concerned with the task and not with relationships.

Go to the next page for feedback.

FEEDBACK ◄────────────────────────

a **You chose (a):** *Your foreman does not understand the nature of the LPC score. He assumes that a high LPC person will always behave in the same way, and, therefore, that LPC can't be any good.* This is most likely the right answer. The foreman did not correctly understand the nature of the LPC score. It measures the importance a person assigns to task and interpersonal goals, and not specific behaviors. As you may remember, in some situations high LPC people do not get along with their subordinates because they become too absorbed in trying to please their boss. In relaxed, well-controlled situations, high LPC leaders sometimes work hard and concentrate on the task. At other times, in situations of moderate control, they are more concerned with interpersonal relationships.

The foreman mistakenly assumed that high LPC leaders always behave in the same way. In addition, of course, it is very difficult to see one's own behavior clearly. Most people are surprised when they learn how others describe them. Therefore, although he may have felt he did not typify a high LPC leader, his goals or motivational system (and his behavior as seen by others) was typical of the high LPC individual.

Turn to page 17 and complete Probe 3.

b **You chose (b):** *Your foreman's score is probably in error since he works hard and is concerned with the task. This suggests that he is more likely to be low LPC.* This answer is not correct. High LPC leaders also are concerned with the task, otherwise they would not be successful in any situation. Moreover, neither high LPC people nor anyone else can necessarily "get along with everybody." In fact, in situations in which they have a high degree of control, high LPC people are sometimes seen as bossy and arrogant. In these situations they also pay a good deal of attention to the task, although they are not necessarily most effective. The points made by the foreman would certainly not be sufficient to think that his LPC score was in error or that it is not a good measure. Reread the descriptions of the two styles of leaders on pages 9-12 and then try Probe 2 again. (Use a bookmark to hold your place at Probe 2.)

c **You chose (c):** *The foreman probably misunderstood the scoring system. A person with a high LPC score is more concerned with the task and not with interpersonal relationships.* This is incorrect. A high LPC score *does* indicate concern with interpersonal relationships while a low LPC leader is more concerned with task accomplishment. Therefore, the foreman did not misunderstand the scoring of the LPC scale.

You missed on this one, try Probe 2 again after rereading the descriptions on the two styles of leaders on pages 9-12. (Use a bookmark to hold your place at Probe 2.)

————————————————————————→ **PROBE 3**

Your supervisor is generally a very relaxed person, especially as long as he has everything under control. However, since he got a new boss, you have noticed a change in him. You now find that he has really tightened up on discipline. He immediately wants to take formal action against anyone who does not shape up. He also has become very directive and goes around issuing orders. He is likely to be:

___1___ (a) Relationship-motivated.

___2___ (b) Task-motivated.

Go to page 18 for feedback.

FEEDBACK ←――――――――――――――――

(a) **You answered (a):** *Relationship-motivated.* This is not correct. The relationship-motivated leader under the stress of having to adjust to a new boss would tend to seek the support of his co-workers and subordinates and he would be less concerned with the task.

Better review Chapter Two and try Probe 3 again.

(b) **You answered (b):** *Task-motivated.* This is quite correct. The supervisor is likely to be task-motivated. You probably recognized this from several parts of the description. First, the supervisor was quite relaxed when he felt in control. Low LPC leaders are indeed relaxed when they know that the job will be accomplished. They can then take it easy and let things take their course. Secondly, a new boss poses a threat. The supervisor does not know what demands the new boss will make; he does not know how he will get along with the new boss; and what kinds of assignments or standards he will have to live with. Finally, your supervisor became very directive. This is his way of dealing with the problem of a new boss — tightening up his control and discipline.

High LPC leaders would react quite differently. When they are faced with having to relate to a new boss they need the emotional support of their group members and they will, therefore, let up on discipline to avoid antagonizing the group members.

You're doing well; continue on to the next probe on page 19.

→ **PROBE 4**

Larry Berger has been office manager for two years. He has been known as a guy who didn't let his people get away with too much: he kept an eye on things, and he did not hesitate to reprimand people when they deserved it. He also tended to be somewhat aloof from his subordinates and spent a lot of time with his boss.

He recently was transferred to a new office where he has a similar job but somewhat more responsibility and less control over his situation. Interestingly enough, he now seems to be unwilling to maintain any discipline, he doesn't want to give any reprimands or take any other action. He also has become much more friendly with his subordinates. You would diagnose him as:

___/___ (a) Relationship-motivated.

_____ (b) Task-motivated.

Go to the next page for feedback.

FEEDBACK ◄──────────────────────────

(a) **You chose (a):** *Relationship-motivated.* You are quite correct here. This is the typical pattern we find in relationship-motivated persons. When all goes well and they enjoy a great deal of control and influence, they can be task-masters and concerned with tight discipline as a means to impress their boss. They also tend under these conditions to neglect their relations with subordinates and become concerned with their boss and others. This causes them to appear aloof and distant to subordinates. However, a new job, and the need to establish positive interpersonal relations with a new boss and new subordinates creates uncertainty and lower situational control in relationship-motivated leaders. They then are very reluctant to alienate their group members, sometimes to the point of letting them get away with infractions which they would never have allowed before.

You seem to understand the two types of leadership style. Please go on to page 21.

(b) **You chose (b):** *Task-motivated.* This is not correct. Task-motivated leaders, as you will recall, become concerned with the task when they are in a low control, less certain situation. Consider the problems new supervisors have on a job: They must establish themselves with their new boss, supervise new subordinates, and learn something about the job. Under these conditions task-motivated leaders become quite concerned with their ability to accomplish the task, and they therefore tighten, not relax, discipline. They also tend to devote all their energies to their task, often to the detriment of their relationships with their employees.

Reread the sections on relationship- and task-motivated persons (pages 9-12) and try Probe 4 again.

SUMMARY

The best way to identify your leadership style is to complete the Least Preferred Co-worker (LPC) scale. The LPC scale describes the relative importance of your various goals, or your motivational system, which results in a different behavior as the situation changes. This summary should be useful to you in reviewing the two different leadership styles.

Relationship-Motivated — High LPC (score of 64 and above)

Generally this kind of leader is more concerned with interpersonal relations, more sensitive to the feelings and needs of others, and tries to head off conflict. They are better able to deal with complex issues in the interpersonal relations area, and are able to take more factors into account when they make personnel decisions.

In high control situations relationship-motivated persons tend to seek the approval and esteem of their superiors. As a result, they usually become somewhat inconsiderate towards their subordinates and more concerned with the performance of the task.

In moderate control situations, relationship-motivated leaders become concerned with interpersonal relations. They seek to alleviate anxiety and tension in their group, they mediate conflict, and they are patient and able to handle creative decision-making groups. They are considerate and concerned with the feelings and opinions of their group members.

In low control situations, relationship-motivated leaders become absorbed by their concern for good interpersonal relations to the detriment of the task. Under extremely stressful situations, they may also withdraw from the leadership role, failing to direct the group's work.

Task-Motivated — Low LPC (score of 57 and below)

Generally, this type of leader is more concerned with the task, and less sensitive to interpersonal relations. They are generally eager and impatient to get on with the job. They quickly organize the job and have a no-nonsense attitude about getting the work done.

In high control situations, task-motivated leaders tend to develop pleasant and comfortable interpersonal relations with subordinates. They are easy to get along with, and as long as the work gets done, they do not interfere nor do they like interference from their superiors.

In moderate control situations, task-motivated leaders tend to be anxious and out of their element. They become engrossed in the task and pay little or no attention to interpersonal relations in the group. They tend to be insensitive to the needs and feelings of their group members and do not head off imminent conflicts within the group.

In low control situations, task-motivated leaders tend to withdraw from interpersonal relations to devote themselves to their challenging task. They organize and drive the group to task-completion. Group members frequently respect this kind of leader for enabling them to reach the group's goal even though the situation may be uncomfortable. Under these conditions, the leader also tends to become concerned with control of the group and maintains strict discipline.

If your score falls into the borderline area, that is, between about 58 and 63, you must carefully weigh whether you belong more in one group or the other.

You have now learned to identify leadership motivations, and you have determined your own leadership style. Remember that no single leadership style is effective in all situations. Rather, certain leadership styles are best suited for some situations but not for others. The next section will discuss how to measure the amount of control various situations give the leader, and how to identify the situations in which you as a leader are likely to perform best.

Now try the Part I Self-Test on the next page.

PART I SELF-TEST

Indicate whether the statements below are true or false.

_____F_____ 1. The leadership styles measured by the LPC scale give a highly stable set of behaviors which do not vary across situations.

_____F_____ 2. Low LPC, task-motivated leaders are generally less well-liked by their followers than are other types of leaders.

_T_ _F_ 3. High LPC, relationship-motivated leaders are primarily motivated to gain esteem from other people.

_T_ _F_ 4. Low LPC leaders are most comfortable in situations where task demands are clear and orderly.

_T_ _F_ 5. High LPC leaders generally try to avoid interpersonal conflict.

_____T_____ 6. In low control situations, low LPC leaders are more critical and directive than high LPC leaders.

_____F_____ 7. Under predictable and relaxed conditions, low LPC leaders are likely to act nervous, edgy, and distracted.

_____T_____ 8. Low LPC leaders tend to be most productive in very high control situations or in very low control situations.

Go to the next page for the answers to this Self-Test.

Answers to Part I Self-Test

False   1. *The leadership styles measured by the LPC scale* **does not** *give a highly stable set of behaviors which do not vary across situations.* Although a leader's needs and motivations will remain relatively constant, different leadership situations present varying opportunities for achievement of these needs. Therefore different leaders use varying strategies or behaviors for satisfying their needs.

False   2. *Low LPC, task-motivated leaders are* **not** *generally less well-liked by their followers than are high LPC leaders.* Both types of leaders have positive and negative points, and are about equally well-liked by their followers.

True   3. *High LPC, relationship-motivated leaders are primarily motivated to gain esteem from other people.* High LPC leaders gain self-esteem when other people (followers, peers, superiors) like them and judge them to be competent.

True   4. *Low LPC leaders are most comfortable in situations where task demands are clear and orderly.* Low LPC leaders do indeed function most effectively and feel most relaxed when the job demands are clear. A clearly defined job gives them a better chance to gain esteem from successful task achievement.

True   5. *High LPC leaders generally try to avoid interpersonal conflict.* By and large, this statement is true. High LPC leaders are sensitive to the interpersonal atmosphere in their group. They try to head off conflict and maintain pleasant work relations.

True   6. *In low control situations low LPC leaders are more critical and directive than high LPC leaders.* When low LPC leaders feel themselves under pressure, they strive to create an orderly task environment. They do this by assigning jobs, directing work, and closely monitoring performance.

False   7. *Under predictable and relaxed conditions, low LPC leaders are* **not** *likely to act nervous, edgy, and distracted.* When situations are clear, predictable, and controllable, low LPC leaders feel relatively assured that they can satisfy their needs. They then become relaxed and considerate with followers.

True   8. *Low LPC leaders tend to be most productive in very high control situations or in very low control situations.* Low LPC leaders seem to perform best under very good conditions when task demands are very clear and they know what to do, and under very uncertain conditions where their directiveness and no-nonsense style gives at least some order to an otherwise chaotic situation.

PART II
Identifying Leadership Situations

CHAPTER THREE

Your Leadership Situation

As we have said, the effectiveness of leaders and their groups depends on two major factors: First is the underlying motivation of leaders, that is, the type of goals which are basically most important to them (leadership style); and second, the degree to which they can control and influence their leadership situation.

There are some leadership situations in which you will be much more effective than in others. Not everybody would be effective in supervising a job which, day-in and day-out, requires tightening bolts on a piece of machinery. Some people not only want variety in their job, but also desire uncertainty and challenge in their assignments. Others are much better in jobs in which they know exactly what they are doing; they like to establish a routine and stick to it. Some leaders perform best under time pressure; some are able to deal well with hostile subordinates; while still others must have peace and quiet.

It is extremely important that you learn to recognize the particular conditions and situations in which you are most effective as a leader, and the conditions which are not your cup of tea. You should not only learn how to recognize these situations but also how to modify them so that they will fit your particular style and leadership approach, thereby maximizing your effectiveness.

What do we mean by "leadership situation?" The underlying basis for classifying a leadership situation is the degree to which it provides leaders with control and influence. This means the extent to which leaders can determine what their group is going to do, and what the outcomes of their actions and decisions are going to be. It also means that the leader can predict with a high degree of certainty and assurance what will happen when he or she wants something done.

There are three major components which primarily determine control and influence in the situation.

1. *Leader-member relations:* The degree to which the group supports the leader.

2. *Task structure:* The degree to which the task clearly spells out goals, procedures, and specific guidelines.

3. *Position power:* The degree to which the position gives the leader authority to reward and punish subordinates.

These dimensions can be combined in various ways to describe the amount of situational control in any leadership position. For example, if a construction superintendent constructs a bridge from a set of blueprints with the full support of his subordinates, he knows with considerable certainty that he can get the job done. The task itself may be difficult but because it is clearly spelled out by the blueprints, the superintendent will have no doubts about the way in which he must go about the job and what the results should look like. In this situation, the construction superintendent has a great deal of control and influence.

In contrast, consider a task such as chairing a Parent-Teachers Association committee to organize a picnic that "everybody will enjoy." Here the task itself may seem easy but the leader has very little control. The group members are likely to be volunteers who can, if they want, walk out on the committee at any time. The chairperson has no power to make them work, and how can you predict in advance whether everybody will enjoy the picnic?

These three components are used to measure the amount of control in a leadership situation. The leadership situation is then divided into three areas: high control, moderate control, or low control. An example of a high control situation would be that of the construction superintendent who builds bridges. He has a great deal of control and influence in his situation because he can be reasonably certain that (a) his subordinates will willingly follow his instructions because he has their full support, (b) he can fire those who fail to do what they are told, and (c) he has a set of specifications and blueprints which tell him exactly how to proceed and what the final product should look like.

The chairperson of the picnic committee, on the other hand, has no such assurances; his or her situation, therefore would be low in control. An example of a moderate control situation would be the leader of a research team developing new products. In this situation the leader may have the support of the team, but no one can predict the best procedure or the final product. Also, a team leader can't fire or discipline scientists on whom he or she must depend for creative research. Therefore, his or her control is moderate.

Before you begin the actual measurement of these three important components, read the brief descriptions of each on the following pages and try your hand at the probes.

LEADER-MEMBER RELATIONS

The *most important* single element in situational control is the amount of loyalty, dependability, and support you, as the leader, get from those with whom you work. If the group is sincerely trying to assist you in getting the job done, and to follow your directions and policies in spirit as well as in letter, your control will be quite high. If you have the group's support then you need not depend on your position power or task structure to get compliance; the group members already accept your direction. Such a leadership situation, is, therefore, likely to give you either high or moderate control.

Conflict with the group demands a great deal of time and effort. If you are the leader of an antagonistic group, you must work warily, constantly wondering whether everything is going to work out all right, or even whether somebody is trying to sabotage your efforts. When you are unsure about your group's loyalty and dependability, you must be on your guard and rely more heavily on position power and the structure of the task in order to get the job accomplished.

Also important is the support you get from your boss. If your boss accepts and supports you, the group members are more likely to hold you in esteem, and to accept your leadership. Moreover, if your recommendations to your boss are accepted and approved, your members will have more confidence in you as their leader. For some leaders this is one of the most important aspects of a leadership situation.

TASK STRUCTURE

The second most important dimension concerns the structure of the task. How clearly is it spelled out, are the goals known, is there a clear and accepted procedure for performing the job? Some tasks or assignments are spelled out in considerable detail and in a way which allows little or no deviation.

To go back to an earlier example, building a bridge would be a highly structured task. The construction superintendent will have a set of detailed instructions, specifications, and drawings which must be followed. At certain points along the way the work will be inspected and approved, and final engineering tests will determine whether the bridge is ready for use.

In contrast, a school picnic can be organized in innumerable ways. No one can predict whether a particular plan will be successful or unsuccessful until after it is too late. And there are certainly few generally accepted methods and no infallible rules for organizing a picnic. This is, therefore, an unstructured task as is every task which requires creativity, important decision-making, and lacks detailed guidelines. Task structure is perhaps the most complex of the three dimensions which make up situational control.

POSITION POWER

The third element in determining your situational control is the power which the organization vests in your leadership position for the purpose of directing subordinates. You will usually find high position power in line jobs of most military, business, and industrial organizations. These typically include foremen, line managers, and supervisors who direct work which involves routine production-oriented tasks. It also includes most military leaders with middle or lower level command responsibilities.

As the chairperson of a committee or the leader of a group performing creative or nonroutine tasks, you will generally have lower position power. Relatively low position power is also found in such organizations as some university departments, advisory boards, or research teams where the members have a strong voice in management, as well as in professional organizations where the leader must depend on senior employees for advice and assistance. It is, after all, very difficult to lean too hard on such key subordinates as your legal counsel or your chief economist or the only technician who can program your computer.

Again, the support which you enjoy from your superiors is important. If you can get your recommendations accepted, can get your people promoted, or get them good assignments, your power in the eyes of your subordinates will be higher than if you have little or no influence with your own boss. If subordinates can readily go over your head to the next higher level, you will have correspondingly less power.

Although position power is the aspect of situational control which usually comes to mind first, it is the least important of the three which we have discussed and is weighted less in the measurement of situational control. For example, no matter how much power and authority you have, it is hardly ever enough to prevent the sabotage of a group effort by a disgruntled subordinate or to evoke more than the minimal amount of effort from an uncooperative group.

MEASURING SITUATIONAL CONTROL

The next four chapters aim to show you how to assess the situational control of your current leadership job, and of leadership jobs you may be asked to hold in the future. We have developed scales to measure each of the three dimensions which make up situational control: leader-member relations, task structure, and position power.

Before you begin to rate your current leadership job, you should get some practice using each of these scales. For this reason, we ask you to select a leadership job you have held in the past.

Practically everyone has held several leadership jobs in the course of his life. You probably are in a management or leadership position right now. In this case, your *primary leadership job* is the one you hold at this time. You should *not* rate this job until later in the training program. For practice right now, pick some other leadership job, your *secondary leadership job*.

In case you have difficulty deciding what to choose, consider the following: Even if you have never held a formal leadership position as part of a regular job, you have probably been responsible for directing the work of others on many different occasions. You may have been the chairperson of one or more committees in your high school or college; you may have had some leadership responsibilities in a volunteer organization, in scouting, in your church, or in a social club.

Almost every leader or manager has had occasion to direct the work of groups. You may have chaired a committee to look into a particular problem or to arrange a company picnic. These all qualify as leadership jobs even though they were only temporary. If you have never held a leadership job before, consider the time you may have found yourself in charge of a group of people cleaning up after a party, or getting a room ready for a meeting, or organizing a car pool.

If you are not now in a position that involves supervision and direction of the work of others, reserve your most important leadership job in the past as your *primary* job, and use the second most important job in these next four chapters.

It is not important what kind of a leadership situation you choose but that you choose a job that you know and can remember fairly accurately. You should also choose a leadership job in which you supervised more than one person. Write the title of this position on the lines below:

Secondary Leadership Job ___Truck Driver Assistant Foreman___

Remember, in the next four chapters when you are asked to complete scales for your *secondary leadership job*, use the position you listed above.

Now try the probes on the following pages.

If your group supports you, your control and influence will be high.

→ **PROBE 5**

Based on what you have just read about situational control, which of the following statements is *most* accurate?

_____ (a) A leader's influence and control with subordinates is determined primarily by formal organizational authority — position power.

___1___ (b) The structure of the group's task is the most important determinant of the leader's control and influence — task structure.

_____ (c) Leader control is a vague and complex phenomenon which cannot be measured.

___2___ (d) A leader's control is dependent upon several factors in the situation, and most importantly, acceptance by group members — loador mombor rolatione.

Go to page 32 for feedback.

FEEDBACK ←——————————————————————

a You chose (a): *A leader's influence and control with subordinates is determined primarily by formal organizational authority — position power.* This is incorrect. In fact, formal authority is usually less important than other situational factors. As you will recall, a leader's power and authority are rarely great enough to prevent the sabotage of a group effort by a disgruntled subordinate or to evoke more than the minimal amount of effort from an uncooperative group.

Review Chapter Three and try Probe 5 again.

b You chose (b): *The structure of the group's task is the most important determinant of the leader's control and influence — task structure.* This answer is not correct. It is true that a leader's control will be increased to the extent that he or she understand the demands of the task and can assign members to specific duties. However, this is not the most important determinant of the situation.

You had better reread Chapter Three and try Probe 5 again.

c You chose (c): *Leader control is a vague and complex phenomenon which cannot be measured.* This, fortunately, is incorrect. If it were true that the leader's control is so complex that measurement is impossible, this training program also would be impossible. While leadership situations are often vague and complex, and therefore, difficult to classify, we have been able to measure the degree to which they give the leader control and influence.

You've missed the point. Read Chapter Three again; then make another choice of the alternatives given in Probe 5.

d You chose (d): *A leader's control is dependent upon several factors in the situation, and most importantly, acceptance by group members — leader-member relations.* Correct! The influence and control of leaders is increased to the degree that they can count on every person to do their job as well as possible (leader-member relations). This is the most important dimension in determining situational control. The clarity and specificity of job demands (task structure) and the leader's power to recognize and reward good work (position power) combine with leader-member relations to determine the total amount of situational control.

Good work, now try Probe 6 on page 33.

———————————————————————→ **PROBE 6**

A friend of yours who is an executive trainee says that it's easy to be a leader of any group if you have a lot of power to reward and punish the subordinates. She says, "You give me the authority, and there's no way I won't be in control!"

What do you say to her in response to this statement?

_____ (a) You are right. If you have enough power, people will do what you tell them to do and that is leadership control.

___|___ (b) You are wrong. What good is the ability to force people to do something if you can't figure out what they should be doing? Besides, when your subordinates don't like you, they can usually figure out some way to "do you in" regardless of how much power you have.

_____ (c) You are wrong. It's not power that counts, it's personality. If your subordinates like you, you'll be successful.

Turn to the next page for feedback.

FEEDBACK ←——————————————————————————

(a) **You chose (a):** *Right. If you have enough power, people will do what you tell them to do and that is leadership control.* This answer is incorrect. Sometimes force can be useful for a leader, but this simplistic approach overlooks the fact that leadership is a lot more complicated than just ordering people around. Imagine being the leader of a Board of Inquiry. Could you use your power to force the members to vote your way?

Reread the section describing the three components of situational control (pages 27-29) and make another choice in Probe 6.

(b) **You chose (b):** *Wrong. What good is the ability to force people to do something if you can't figure out what they should be doing? Besides, when your subordinates don't like you, they can figure out some way to "do you in" regardless of how much power you have.* Right you are. True leadership control is certainty about what should be done and certainty that your subordinates are willing to help you do it. It is far more complicated than just being able to order people around.

Good work; continue on page 35.

(c) **You chose (c):** *Wrong. It's not power that counts, it's personality. If your subordinates like you, you'll be successful.* This answer is not correct. Good relations with subordinates are extremely important in a leadership position, but it is an oversimplification to think that that is the whole story. The relationship between leaders and their followers involves more than just being liked. Remember the key words in our discussion are control and influence. Being a nice person might give you more control and influence in your situation but it won't help if nobody knows how to do the job, or if it means letting people do their own thing rather than doing their job.

Make another choice in Probe 6 — you've missed the point!

SUMMARY

In this chapter you were introduced to the term "situational control" which describes how much control and influence you have over your leadership situation. The three components of situational control are:

1. *Leader-Member Relations:* The degree to which the group supports the leader.

2. *Task Structure:* The degree to which the task clearly spells out goals, procedures, and specific guidelines.

3. *Position Power:* The degree to which the position gives the leader the authority to reward and punish subordinates.

The next chapter describes in detail the measurement of leader-member relations.

CHAPTER FOUR

Measuring Leader-Member Relations

Leadership implies control and influence over others. Your control and influence obviously will be greater if you have the support and trust of your group members than if the group rejects you or gives you only half-hearted support. Not having to worry about the dependability and loyalty of your group members puts you in a very strong position and gives you considerable control over your situation. In other words, you don't have to rely as much on your official power or other organizational supports as union contracts, organizational rules, or the chain of command. You also don't have to rely on your power to reward and punish because the group members are eager to follow you anyway. We speak of this personal aspect of leader control and influence as *leader-member relations.*

Leader-member relations are the *most important* single aspect of situational control. Good relations and support from your group assure you of either high or moderate situational control. While leaders who have good relations with their group members are not necessarily more effective, they are clearly more influential, and their group members generally are more satisfied with their jobs.

Unfortunately, it is sometimes rather difficult to tell just how much support and backing a group is likely to give you. Most of us have a tendency to do some wishful thinking in this area; we like to believe that our relations are better than they actually are.

Various clues may help you assess the extent to which subordinates accept your direction. For example:

* Do your group members try to keep you out of trouble?

* Do they warn you about potential difficulties?

* Are they conscientious about how they do their job?

* Do they do what you want them to do rather than just what you tell them to do?

* Do they include you in their small talk?

* Do they seem genuinely friendly and eager to please you?

If you can answer most of these questions with "yes" then your relations with your subordinates are probably good.

Other factors affect your relations with the group. Groups in which there is considerable conflict, whether caused by personality clashes or by differences in values, background, or language, are difficult to handle. You may be seen as favoring one clique over another, or you may be mistrusted by the members who are from a different cultural background. However, in many organizations, cultural differences are taken for granted and so such differences play a minor role.

Another factor to consider is the group's history. Some groups traditionally have good relations with their leaders while others traditionally fight their leaders. Also, if the leader who preceded you on your job was liked and admired, it will probably be more difficult to step into his shoes. If the leader before you was a disaster, you may find it easier to be accepted or you may find that the members are mistrustful and it may take longer to establish good relations.

Also important is your relationship with your boss. If your boss supports you and works with you, the group members are more likely to hold you in esteem. Moreover, if your recommendations to your boss are accepted and approved, your members will have more confidence in you as their leader.

The leader-member relations scale (LMR) has been designed to take all these factors into consideration. Because leader-member relations are the most important dimension in measuring situational control, the scale has been weighted to be worth a maximum of forty points, or twice as much as the task structure scale and four times as much as the position power scale. The LMR scale consists of eight questions with response choices ranging from "strongly agree" to "strongly disagree." Circle the number which best represents your feelings about each question. The scale is scored by adding the circled numbers and entering the total at the bottom of the scale.

Practice using this scale by completing the two probes on the following pages. Respond as if you are the leader of the group in question. Completed scales are provided with the feedback for each job, so you can compare your rating with ours. If your ratings come out within 2 or 3 points of ours, you are well within the acceptable range.

───► PROBE 7

You are the supervisor of the office staff of a small insurance company. You have been in this position for six years and your nine employees have been with you for varying periods from six months to four years. The office runs very smoothly and there have been no complaints from the senior staff about the quality of the work. The nice thing about this group is that you can assign work and know that it will get completed on time and correctly. This has the effect of freeing you from close supervision and allows you to work on other aspects of your job.

You have lunch with your employees at least once a week and spend an occasional evening in their company. You have noticed, however, that there is some competition among the group and relations between them are sometimes strained. You have discussed this problem with your boss and he has indicated he will support any actions you take. So far, the situation has not gotten out of hand and it has not interfered with group productivity.

You estimate the leader-member relations of your group to be:

_____✓_ Good

_____ Moderate

_____ Poor

Now complete the LMR scale on the following page to see how well you have estimated.

LEADER-MEMBER RELATIONS SCALE

Circle the number which best represents your response to each item.

	strongly agree	agree	neither agree nor disagree	disagree	strongly disagree
1. The people I supervise have trouble getting along with each other.	1	②	3	4	5
2. My subordinates are reliable and trustworthy.	⑤	4	3	2	1
3. There seems to be a friendly atmosphere among the people I supervise.	5	④	3	2	1
4. My subordinates always cooperate with me in getting the job done.	5	④	3	2	1
5. There is friction between my subordinates and myself.	1	2	3	④	5
6. My subordinates give me a good deal of help and support in getting the job done.	5	4	③	2	1
7. The people I supervise work well together in getting the job done.	5	④	3	2	1
8. I have good relations with the people I supervise.	5	④	3	2	1

Total Score 30

FEEDBACK ←——————————

LEADER-MEMBER RELATIONS SCALE

Circle the number which best represents your response to each item.

	strongly agree	agree	neither agree nor disagree	disagree	strongly disagree
1. The people I supervise have trouble getting along with each other.	1	2	(3)	4	5
2. My subordinates are reliable and trustworthy.	(5)	4	3	2	1
3. There seems to be a friendly atmosphere among the people I supervise.	5	4	(3)	2	1
4. My subordinates always cooperate with me in getting the job done.	(5)	4	3	2	1
5. There is friction between my subordinates and myself.	1	2	3	4	(5)
6. My subordinates give me a good deal of help and support in getting the job done.	(5)	4	3	2	1
7. The people I supervise work well together in getting the job done.	5	4	(3)	2	1
8. I have good relations with the people I supervise.	(5)	4	3	2	1

Total Score   **34**

FEEDBACK ←————————————————————

As you probably estimated, the leader-member relations in this situation were good. If you have a scale value in the vicinity of 34, you are in the right range. The fact that there is some competition between the group members would mean that you should probably have answered items 1, 3, and 7 as "neither agree nor disagree." They obviously don't have trouble getting along most of the time or they wouldn't get the job done and you wouldn't feel as confident in "freeing yourself from close supervision." So choosing the answer in the middle would, most likely, represent the situation accurately. Because your relations with them are good, their occasional conflict would not effectively lower your LMR score.

A score of 25 or above on the LMR scale indicates good leader-member relations, a score of 20-25 indicates moderate leader-member relations, and a score below 20 indicates poor leader-member relations.

Try Probe 8 on the following page.

—————————————————————————▶ **PROBE 8**

You are a supervisor for the Ding Dong Telephone Company in one of the smaller rural districts. Your primary responsibility is to supervise the 22 telephone operators and 6 information operators to provide service for the community. You have recently been transferred to this district from a similar job in a major city and feel a lot of pressure from your new boss to keep things running smoothly. However, most of the operators in your shift have been at their jobs for a number of years and strongly resent having an outsider brought in to replace their former boss with whom they had worked a long time.

You feel that much could be done to improve the phone service by using more modern methods. Most of your employees are unwilling to take suggestions from you regarding their phone contacts with the public. Several of the newer operators have been trying to persuade the group to cooperate and this has caused a lot of trouble and tension. Several angry arguments have occurred among the group members and between you and your staff.

You estimate your leader-member relations to be

_____ Good

_____ Moderate

___✓__ Poor

Now complete the LMR scale for this job on the following page.

LEADER-MEMBER RELATIONS SCALE

Circle the number which best represents your response to each item.

	strongly agree	agree	neither agree nor disagree	disagree	strongly disagree
1. The people I supervise have trouble getting along with each other.	1	2	(3)	4	5
2. My subordinates are reliable and trustworthy.	5	(4)	3	2	1
3. There seems to be a friendly atmosphere among the people I supervise.	5	4	(3)	2	1
4. My subordinates always cooperate with me in getting the job done.	5	4	3	2	(1)
5. There is friction between my subordinates and myself.	(1)	2	3	4	5
6. My subordinates give me a good deal of help and support in getting the job done.	5	4	3	2	(1)
7. The people I supervise work well together in getting the job done.	5	4	(3)	2	1
8. I have good relations with the people I supervise.	5	4	3	(2)	1

Total Score 18

FEEDBACK ◄━━━━━━━━━━━━━━

LEADER-MEMBER RELATIONS SCALE

Circle the number which best represents your response to each item.

	strongly agree	agree	neither agree nor disagree	disagree	strongly disagree
1. The people I supervise have trouble getting along with each other.	①︎	2	3	4	5
2. My subordinates are reliable and trustworthy.	5	4	3	②︎	1
3. There seems to be a friendly atmosphere among the people I supervise.	5	4	3	②︎	1
4. My subordinates always cooperate with me in getting the job done.	5	4	3	②︎	1
5. There is friction between my subordinates and myself.	①︎	2	3	4	5
6. My subordinates give me a good deal of help and support in getting the job done.	5	4	3	2	①︎
7. The people I supervise work well together in getting the job done.	5	4	3	2	①︎
8. I have good relations with the people I supervise.	5	4	3	2	①︎

Total Score

FEEDBACK ◄───────────────────

Obviously this leadership situation has poor leader-member relations. As you can see from the feedback scale, a total of 11 would be appropriate. However, if your score is less than 20, you got this one right.

In a situation where your employees don't support and trust you, and there is dissension among them, your control and influence over the group is going to be either low or, at best, moderate. This situation is, of course, an extreme one but it does give you an opportunity to look at the scale from a less positive viewpoint.

Now that you have had some experience completing the LMR scale, complete the scale on the following page for your secondary leadership situation, that is, the job you chose for practice. Your score on this scale will then be used later in the program to determine your total situational control score for this secondary leadership job. After completing the scale, go on to the summary.

LEADER-MEMBER RELATIONS SCALE

Circle the number which best represents your response to each item.

	strongly agree	agree	neither agree nor disagree	disagree	strongly disagree
1. The people I supervise have trouble getting along with each other.	1	2	(3)	4	5
2. My subordinates are reliable and trustworthy.	5	4	3	(2)	1
3. There seems to be a friendly atmosphere among the people I supervise.	5	(4)	3	2	1
4. My subordinates always cooperate with me in getting the job done.	5	4	3	(2)	1
5. There is friction between my subordinates and myself.	1	2	(3)	4	5
6. My subordinates give me a good deal of help and support in getting the job done.	5	(4)	3	2	1
7. The people I supervise work well together in getting the job done.	5	(4)	3	2	1
8. I have good relations with the people I supervise.	5	4	(3)	2	1

Total Score 25

SUMMARY

Leaders' relations with group members are the most important single factor in determining situational control. If you have the support of your group, if you can rely on group members to do their job well and willingly, then you have a considerable degree of control and influence. This is true even if your formal power to reward and punish is relatively slight or if your task is low in structure.

This chapter introduced the leader-member relations (LMR) scale. You should recognize that a scale of this type can be no better than your own sensitivity to the group members' relations with you and with each other. For this reason, you should make a practice of observing your group in action as often as possible so that you can accurately assess your leader-member relations.

In particular, there are two major components which you need to watch for:

• The support you get from your subordinates.

• The relationship among the members of your group, including the possibility of conflict and dissension between them.

CHAPTER FIVE

Measuring Task Structure

The second step in determining situational control is to measure task structure. You normally don't think of the task or the nature of the job as directly affecting your control and influence. However, consider the case of a construction foreman, who says to his men, "I guess they want us to build a storage shed someplace around here, so let's see what we can do."

In effect, this foreman tells his members that he doesn't know exactly what to do and invites the crew to argue about the nature and placement of the shed. If the same foreman has a blueprint in his hand which tells him exactly how to build the storage shed and where to place it, he will get no arguments from his crew.

The job "to build a shed someplace around here" may later be criticized by the foreman's boss for not being built in the right way or in the right spot. There is no such uncertainty when the blueprint specifies the location and method of building. Leaders, therefore, have more situational control if their task is highly structured and they know what is to be done.

Being told exactly what to do and how to do it relieves leaders from the uncertainty of outcome which goes with making decisions on their own. It tells the group in effect that the supervisor knows exactly what is supposed to be done, and that he or she has the full backing of the organization for doing the work in the approved manner. The well-known military method of "doing things by the numbers" may not always be the most efficient, but it is the equivalent of the blueprint, as is the standard operating procedure in business and industry. In each of these cases leaders have more control over the job being done and their subordinates are less likely to question their authority.

A quite different situation exists in jobs where the nature of the task simply cannot be reduced to a step-by-step procedure, and where the outcome may not be known until well after the task is completed or, in some cases, only years later. Let us take, for example, the job of a public relations director. This job is creative and involves supervising creative people. If he is asked to design a publicity campaign, he will probably brainstorm with his staff to find a solution to the problem. Each member of his staff may have some good ideas and some ideas which may prove worthless. There is no way to tell which approach will succeed and which will fail — and the outcome may not be known for months or years after the job is completed.

Likewise, the director of a research laboratory has a very unstructured task. It is extremely difficult to predict which line of research will turn into a blind alley, and which will lead to a marketable product. Every wrong turn carries a high cost in time and money. Again, the outcome may remain uncertain for several years, there are few rules to follow, there are no "best" procedures in developing a research program, and the risk of failure is high. As a result, it is hard for the research director to say to the group that he is right and they are wrong. The members of a research staff must constantly use their own judgment, and the director of the group cannot supervise and control every step of the project. The supervisor of a highly unstructured task can exercise only nominal control over the way the task is performed.

As we said earlier, task structure is second in importance to leader-member relations and is more difficult to measure. To measure task structure, we have developed a two-part scale. Part 1 is based on the aspects of task structure discussed next. Part 2 involves the effect of training and experience on task structure and will be discussed in more detail later in this chapter. As with the Leader-Member Relations scale, this scale has been weighted to reflect its importance in measuring situational control. The maximum score possible on the task structure scale is 20, half as much as the LMR scale.

ASPECTS OF TASK STRUCTURE

To measure task structure, we examine four aspects of the job:

Is the goal or outcome clearly stated or known? How clearly are the requirements of your job (the tasks or duties which typically constitute your job) stated or known to you? For example, consider how your directions are given: repair this car so that it runs again, paint this building white; or, develop a new training program, write a policy statement.

Is there only one way to accomplish the task? If the problems encountered in your job can be solved by one or two methods, the task is more structured than if a wide variety of procedures are possible. For example, the supervisor of an axle assembly line in an auto manufacturing plant insures that the workers bolt front or rear axle assemblies to a chassis. This can be done correctly in only one way. However, a research engineer whose job calls for improving or discovering new products, has any number of ways to proceed. Therefore, the job is *low* in task structure.

Is there only one correct answer or solution possible for completing the task? If there is only one "correct solution" for a task, it is more highly structured than if many solutions are possible. Some tasks, for example, arithmetic problems, have only one correct answer; others have two or more, like sorting clothing by color, by size, or by material. Still other tasks have an infinite number of possible solutions or outcomes, for instance, the development of a short story, or designing a recruiting display.

How easy is it to check whether the job was done right? You have to consider the degree to which it is possible to determine the "correctness" of the solution or of the decisions which you make in the performance of your job. If you build a structure, you can check the dimensions of the building against the specifications on the blueprint. If you assemble a machine, you can determine how well it performs. If you estimate the number of people who live in a district, you can check your estimate against the latest census data. These kinds of tasks are *higher* in structure.

For some jobs, however, it is difficult to know whether the outcome was good or bad, whether your group performed well or poorly. A group of economists may come to an agreement that a cut in taxes will create more jobs . . . "other things being equal," but it may never be possible to establish if they are right. You may be responsible for developing a new policy on job rotation for your company but it will be difficult to determine whether the system is effective. These jobs are *lower* in task structure.

Also important is whether you can get feedback on the results of your work. Are there milestones and benchmarks along the way? Can you see whether you are making right or wrong decisions? A builder can check whether various requirements have been met, a construction engineer can conduct stress tests, a production manager can institute various quality controls at important points in the process. All of these are highly structured tasks.

Other jobs do not allow this. For the scriptwriting team working on a new training film there is no way to tell in advance whether the audience will learn from the film or be bored by it. Consider the general who will not know the success of the campaign plan until it is too late to do anything about it. These situations are lower in structure.

Part 1 of the Task Structure Scale is designed to reflect these aspects of task structure. It consists of ten questions with response choices of "Usually," "Sometimes," or "Seldom," and each choice is assigned a value ranging from 0 to 2.

Most of the questions are fairly straightforward and are representative of the four dimensions of task structure discussed above. However, a couple of questions may cause you some difficulty. Question 2, for example, asks, "Is there a person available to advise and give a description of the finished product or service, or how the job should be done?" This can be anyone from your boss to a subordinate or even the person who had the job before. The important point is not who the person is but rather whether there is someone who can help clarify the job with *detailed instructions.*

Question 8 asks "Is there a generally agreed understanding about the standards the particular product or service has to meet to be considered acceptable?" For example, the standards for repairing a car involve whether the car will run correctly after the repair work is done. The standards for training apprentices how to clean and care for a piece of machinery are clearly specified. On the other hand, planning a program to improve community relations is rather open-ended, and even where particular standards for the program are spelled out, a great deal of leeway exists. In other words, reasonable people may well arrive at quite different judgments and conclusions. It is often difficult, therefore, to tell when this kind of task has been accomplished effectively.

You may have trouble with Question 9 which relates to the previous and asks, "Is the evaluation of this task generally made on some quantitative basis?" In other words, when the task has been completed, can it be rated by different people with good agreement on a fairly standardized basis? For example, the USDA meat rating system, a city plumbing code, or an aircraft inspection checklist, are all quantitative systems for evaluating tasks. Rating the performance of an orchestra is not.

Read each question on the scale carefully and circle the number which best represents your choice. Keep in mind the various examples on the preceding pages which illustrate each of these important dimensions. If you have trouble answering a particular question, refer back to the discussion of that dimension for clarification. After completing the scale, add the circled responses and enter the total in the box marked "Subtotal." Remember that this is only the first part of the total task-structure score.

On the pages which follow, are three jobs to be rated on Part 1 of the Task Structure scale. A completed scale is provided with the feedback for each job. If your ratings come out within 2 or 3 points of the score given in the feedback, you are well within the acceptable range.

There are some ways which are clearly recognized as better than others for performing certain tasks.

 **PROBE 9**

Director of Public Relations of the Magnum Opus Corporation The director and his staff have responsibility for developing and maintaining the company's positive image. His team uses available information channels to reach the public with the company's story. He has the responsibility for advising the company on the public relations impact of various courses of action.

Estimate the task structure of the job:

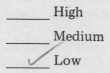

_____ High

_____ Medium

___✓___ Low

Now rate the job on the task structure rating scale on the following page.

TASK STRUCTURE RATING SCALE — PART I

Circle the number in the appropriate column.	Usually True	Sometimes True	Seldom True
Is the Goal Clearly Stated or Known?			
1. Is there a blueprint, picture, model or detailed description available of the finished product or service?	2	(1)	0
2. Is there a person available to advise and give a description of the finished product or service, or how the job should be done?	2	1	(0)
Is There Only One Way to Accomplish the Task?			
3. Is there a step-by-step procedure, or a standard operating procedure which indicates in detail the process which is to be followed?	2	1	(0)
4. Is there a specific way to subdivide the task into separate parts or steps?	2	(1)	0
5. Are there some ways which are clearly recognized as better than others for performing this task?	2	(1)	0
Is There Only One Correct Answer or Solution?			
6. Is it obvious when the task is finished and the correct solution has been found?	2	1	(0)
7. Is there a book, manual, or job description which indicates the best solution or the best outcome for the task?	2	1	(0)
Is It Easy to Check Whether the Job Was Done Right?			
8. Is there a generally agreed understanding about the standards the particular product or service has to meet to be considered acceptable?	2	(1)	0
9. Is the evaluation of this task generally made on some quantitative basis?	2	1	(0)
10. Can the leader and the group find out how well the task has been accomplished in enough time to improve future performance?	2	1	(0)

SUBTOTAL 4

FEEDBACK ◄─────────────────

TASK STRUCTURE RATING SCALE — PART I

Circle the number in the appropriate column.	Usually True	Sometimes True	Seldom True
Is the Goal Clearly Stated or Known?			
1. Is there a blueprint, picture, model or detailed description available of the finished product or service?	2	1	**(0)**
2. Is there a person available to advise and give a description of the finished product or service, or how the job should be done?	2	**(1)**	0
Is There Only One Way to Accomplish the Task?			
3. Is there a step-by-step procedure, or a standard operating procedure which indicates in detail the process which is to be followed?	2	1	**(0)**
4. Is there a specific way to subdivide the task into separate parts or steps?	2	1	**(0)**
5. Are there some ways which are clearly recognized as better than others for performing this task?	2	**(1)**	0
Is There Only One Correct Answer or Solution?			
6. Is is obvious when the task is finished and the correct solution has been found?	2	1	**(0)**
7. Is there a book, manual, or job description which indicates the best solution or the best outcome for the task?	2	1	**(0)**
Is It Easy to Check Whether the Job Was Done Right?			
8. Is there a generally agreed understanding about the standards the particular product or service has to meet to be considered acceptable?	2	**(1)**	0
9. Is the evaluation of this task generally made on some quantitative basis?	2	1	**(0)**
10. Can the leader and the group find out how well the task has been accomplished in enough time to improve future performance?	2	1	**(0)**

SUBTOTAL | 3 |

FEEDBACK ◄─────────────────────────────

The job of Public Relations Director would receive a score of about 3 on the task structure scale. This would mean the job is low in task structure. A score of 6 or below is low in structure, a score between 7 and 13 is medium in structure and a score of 14 or above is high in task structure. The total number of points possible is 20. As with the leader-member relations scale in the previous chapter, this scale has been weighted to reflect its importance in determining situational control. Since task structure is second in importance to leader-member relations, it is worth half the number of points.

How well were you able to estimate the structure of this job? The Public Relations Director's job is very low in structure since there is no clear way to maintain a public image. There are no guidelines, blueprints, or detailed directions. There are many ways to accomplish the task and it is hard to check whether the job was done right.

Question 2 should have been answered with "sometimes" since the director probably has a superior who could give detailed advice. Question 5 was worth one point since "sometimes" there are ways to proceed which are recognized as better than others. Question 8 was also worth one point since it is generally understood that the job is done right as long as the company image stays high. The rest of the questions should have been answered with "seldom". If you came up with a score within 2 or 3 points of the suggested score, you are catching on. If you missed this one, go back to pages 48-51 and review the discussion of task structure. Then try the next probe and see how well you do.

→ **PROBE 10**

Service Manager in charge of motor pool maintenance for Muddy Trail Bus Lines The job requires that vehicles be kept in running order and available for authorized use. In addition, routine scheduled maintenance must be carried out, such as oil changes, filter changes, lubrication.

Estimate the task structure of this job:

_____ High

_____ Medium

_____ Low

Complete the task structure scale on the following page.

TASK STRUCTURE RATING SCALE — PART I

Circle the number in the appropriate column.	Usually True	Sometimes True	Seldom True
Is the Goal Clearly Stated or Known?			
1. Is there a blueprint, picture, model or detailed description available of the finished product or service?	(2)	1	0
2. Is there a person available to advise and give a description of the finished product or service, or how the job should be done?	(2)	1	0
Is There Only One Way to Accomplish the Task?			
3. Is there a step-by-step procedure, or a standard operating procedure which indicates in detail the process which is to be followed?	(2)	1	0
4. Is there a specific way to subdivide the task into separate parts or steps?	2	(1)	0
5. Are there some ways which are clearly recognized as better than others for performing this task?	(2)	1	0
Is There Only One Correct Answer or Solution?			
6. Is it obvious when the task is finished and the correct solution has been found?	(2)	1	0
7. Is there a book, manual, or job description which indicates the best solution or the best outcome for the task?	(2)	1	0
Is It Easy to Check Whether the Job Was Done Right?			
8. Is there a generally agreed understanding about the standards the particular product or service has to meet to be considered acceptable?	(2)	1	0
9. Is the evaluation of this task generally made on some quantitative basis?	2	(1)	0
10. Can the leader and the group find out how well the task has been accomplished in enough time to improve future performance?	(2)	1	0

SUBTOTAL **18**

FEEDBACK ←——————————————————————

TASK STRUCTURE RATING SCALE — PART I

Circle the number in the appropriate column.	Usually True	Sometimes True	Seldom True
Is the Goal Clearly Stated or Known?			
1. Is there a blueprint, picture, model or detailed description available of the finished product or service?	(2)	1	0
2. Is there a person available to advise and give a description of the finished product or service, or how the job should be done?	(2)	1	0
Is There Only One Way to Accomplish the Task?			
3. Is there a step-by-step procedure, or a standard operating procedure which indicates in detail the process which is to be followed?	(2)	1	0
4. Is there a specific way to subdivide the task into separate parts or steps?	(2)	1	0
5. Are there some ways which are clearly recognized as better than others for performing this task?	(2)	1	0
Is There Only One Correct Answer or Solution?			
6. Is is obvious when the task is finished and the correct solution has been found?	(2)	1	0
7. Is there a book, manual, or job description which indicates the best solution or the best outcome for the task?	(2)	1	0
Is It Easy to Check Whether the Job Was Done Right?			
8. Is there a generally agreed understanding about the standards the particular product or service has to meet to be considered acceptable?	(2)	1	0
9. Is the evaluation of this task generally made on some quantitative basis?	2	1	(0)
10. Can the leader and the group find out how well the task has been accomplished in enough time to improve future performance?	(2)	1	0

SUBTOTAL |18|

FEEDBACK ◄─────────────────────

If you estimated this job as high in task structure, you are doing well. A score of 14 or above indicates that the job is high in structure and this one scored 18. Compare this with your rating and see how close you came.

This job is so highly structured that it received the most points for every question except Question 9. This question was answered "seldom" since a quantitative evaluation is rarely made. Generally, if the vehicles are running that's all that counts.

If you came close to 18, you are doing well and should move on to Probe 11 on the next page. If you are still having trouble, you should review this chapter before trying Probe 11.

PROBE 11

Plant Security Chief Duties include supervision of 20 to 30 security personnel, planning, directing, and supervising all phases of the plant security system. Meets with administrative staff and local law enforcement agencies
regarding mutual problems; provides assistance upon request. Develops
training programs to provide a competent security staff; schedules their
supervisory shift assignments; hires personnel. Investigates complaints and
reported violations of plant security regulations. Must be prepared and alert
for any extraordinary or emergency situations involving plant security.

Estimate the task structure of this job.

_____High

___✓___Medium

_____Low

Now rate this job on the task structure rating scale on the following page.

TASK STRUCTURE RATING SCALE — PART I

Circle the number in the appropriate column.	Usually True	Sometimes True	Seldom True
Is the Goal Clearly Stated or Known?			
1. Is there a blueprint, picture, model or detailed description available of the finished product or service?	2	1	(0.)
2. Is there a person available to advise and give a description of the finished product or service, or how the job should be done?	(2)	1	0
Is There Only One Way to Accomplish the Task?			
3. Is there a step-by-step procedure, or a standard operating procedure which indicates in detail the process which is to be followed?	2	(1)	0
4. Is there a specific way to subdivide the task into separate parts or steps?	(2)	1	0
5. Are there some ways which are clearly recognized as better than others for performing this task?	(2)	1	0
Is There Only One Correct Answer or Solution?			
6. Is it obvious when the task is finished and the correct solution has been found?	2	1	(0)
7. Is there a book, manual, or job description which indicates the best solution or the best outcome for the task?	2	1	(0)
Is It Easy to Check Whether the Job Was Done Right?			
8. Is there a generally agreed understanding about the standards the particular product or service has to meet to be considered acceptable?	(2)	1	0
9. Is the evaluation of this task generally made on some quantitative basis?	2	1	(0)
10. Can the leader and the group find out how well the task has been accomplished in enough time to improve future performance?	2	(1)	0

SUBTOTAL | 10 |

FEEDBACK ◄───────────────────────────

TASK STRUCTURE RATING SCALE — PART I

Circle the number in the appropriate column.	Usually True	Sometimes True	Seldom True
Is the Goal Clearly Stated or Known?			
1. Is there a blueprint, picture, model or detailed description available of the finished product or service?	2	1	(0)
2. Is there a person available to advise and give a description of the finished product or service, or how the job should be done?	(2)	1	0
Is There Only One Way to Accomplish the Task?			
3. Is there a step-by-step procedure, or a standard operating procedure which indicates in detail the process which is to be followed?	2	(1)	0
4. Is there a specific way to subdivide the task into separate parts or steps?	(2)	1	0
5. Are there some ways which are clearly recognized as better than others for performing this task?	(2)	1	0
Is There Only One Correct Answer or Solution?			
6. Is is obvious when the task is finished and the correct solution has been found?	2	(1)	0
7. Is there a book, manual, or job description which indicates the best solution or the best outcome for the task?	2	(1)	0
Is It Easy to Check Whether the Job Was Done Right?			
8. Is there a generally agreed understanding about the standards the particular product or service has to meet to be considered acceptable?	2	(1)	0
9. Is the evaluation of this task generally made on some quantitative basis?	2	1	(0)
10. Can the leader and the group find out how well the task has been accomplished in enough time to improve future performance?	2	(1)	0

SUBTOTAL ⬚ **11**

FEEDBACK ←——————————————————————

The plant security chief job occupies a middle point on the task structure dimension. The correct score is around 11. As long as your total score is between 7 and 13, even if you emphasized somewhat different aspects, you are doing well.

Some of the chief's duties are quite clear and covered by rules and guidelines. The highest number of points was awarded for questions 4 and 5. Question 2 also scored highly since the security officer would have a plant manager to turn to for advice and assistance. Some of his duties, however, require making decisions and using his own judgment; therefore, "sometimes" is probably the better answer for questions 3, 6, 7, 8, and 10. Question 1 received no points since there really isn't a blueprint, picture, or model of the finished product, and question 9 received 0 since there is no quantitative basis for measuring how well the job is done.

If your ratings on those three probes don't come close to those shown in the feedback, review pages 48-51 of this chapter before continuing.

If your scores are in the "right ballpark" you are ready to continue on to Part 2 of the scale on the effects of training and experience on task structure, introduced on the next page.

EFFECTS OF LEADERSHIP EXPERIENCE
AND TRAINING ON TASK STRUCTURE

Without adequate leadership training and experience, a leader's task structure is necessarily lower. Therefore, we must adjust the task structure score to reflect lack of experience and training.

Experience and Task Structure

When we speak of leaders with adequate experience, we mean that they have been a leader long enough to learn how to cope with most of the problems which usually confront people in a leadership position. Experience is on-the-job training, and it usually goes along with some coaching by others who are involved with the leader. New leaders are likely to get hints from their superiors, from the person who was in the job before them, and from others in similar positions. They are also likely to get some guidance from the people they supervise. They will be told, for example, that "we always did it this way before," or "you'll find that this method works better."

The highly experienced leader will have faced the same problem time and time again. The work sheets didn't get filled in today, three of the eight people in the department are sick again, Sam and Mike got into an argument over who made the mistake on the last job, and Walt, the new man, is giving you a lot of lip every time he's told to do something.

Experience teaches leaders how to handle these problems. They will no longer get flustered because they've been through all this before. They will know that a call to the accounting department will take care of the time sheet problem and the way to handle Walt is to ignore him, while they need to talk to Sam and Mike like a Dutch uncle.

What this means is that the total situation has become more predictable and more under the control of the leader. The job will seem more structured as time goes by and require fewer new solutions since fewer brand new problems arise. In other words, experience has made the leadership situation more secure, less anxiety-arousing, and consequently under more control.

Effects of Training on Task Structure

Leadership training and experience often are closely related. Most good training tries to reflect the experience of others in integrated and easily digested form. Its main purpose is to make it unnecessary for trainees to figure everything out for themselves. They learn what others have done, and what has, and has not, been effective. By teaching them what has worked for others and letting them practice how to handle various situations, we are in effect trying to make the job more structured. There is less ambiguity about how to perform a task. More guidelines are suggested for telling whether things are proceeding in the right way (easier evaluation) and a better understanding of what is to be accomplished (more goal clarity). Most technical

training will make the persons more competent and, therefore, more know-
ledgeable in their job. They will, therefore, have more control.

A course of training may also "unfreeze" some previous ideas. It may
show leaders alternative ways of doing their job or prepare them to handle
complications specific to the new job. Leaders who have performed well in
the past may learn, through training, that they have overlooked or ignored a
number of aspects in their leadership situation. For example, they may have
ignored the feelings of their subordinates and may have to pay more attention to interpersonal relations with co-workers. However, most training
makes the leader's task more structured and gives more control.

Does Experience and Training Structure
Some Tasks More Than Others?

Some tasks and jobs can be greatly improved by training or by experience.
Others do not benefit from either doing the same job over and over, or from
getting specific instructions on how to do the job. No matter how much we
might train an individual to become an inventor, being inventive is a personal attribute which might be assisted by proper training but cannot be learned.
Likewise, it is difficult to teach anyone how to be a brilliant conductor of
an orchestra, although they can be instructed in the fundamentals of con-
ducting.

Other types of tasks can be readily taught. Generally speaking, the
more structured the task, the more easily it can be taught, and the more
easily we can train a leader or supervisor to direct it. It is relatively easy to
teach an individual how to march men around on a drill field, or how to direct an assembly operation.

The less structured the task, the more judgment is required and the
task becomes more dependent on the leader's creativity or ability to encourage creativity in others. Unstructured tasks, therefore, are less easily improved by training, and the leader will be less likely to benefit from the experience of others.

Most training, and particularly task training, is a method to make tasks
more structured: it provides rules and routines which trainees otherwise
might not know, and presents methods which will assist them in doing the
job without having to create or invent new methods themselves. Without
training a task will, therefore, be seen as less structured.

Measuring the Effects of Training and Experience

Insofar as training and experience affect task structure, we must adjust our
score to reflect this factor. The task structure ratings you read about in the
first part of this chapter are based on the assumption that the leader has had
adequate experience and/or training appropriate for the task. Where leaders
do not have sufficient training and experience, we must then *subtract* points
from the task structure score, since the task will be less structured for the

new than the "old" leader. An additional scale is therefore needed.

(a)   Compared to others in this or similar positions, how much *training* has the leader had?

3	2	1	0
No training at all	Very little training	Moderate amount of training	A great deal of training

(b)   Compared to others in this or similar positions, how much *experience* has the leader had?

6	4	2	0
No experience at all	Very little experience	Moderate amount of experience	A great deal of experience

Since experience seems to be a more powerful influence on task structure, it is assigned more points. However, the rating of training and experience calls upon you to use your judgment. If you do not know or cannot guess the leader's training and experience, mark it as "moderate."

Since extremely unstructured jobs are less affected by experience and training, those jobs with scores below 6 on Part 1 of the Task Structure Rating scale require no adjustment for experience and training.

Without experience and training even structured jobs present problems.

Note that we are talking here about *relevant* training and experience. Thus, if you are promoted to sales manager, training in special sales techniques or the use of advertisements would be relevant. Training in typing would not be relevant. Likewise, experience which is related to the present job, even if indirectly, should be counted.

It is not possible to determine for every leadership position what training or experience is important. You must use your knowledge of each unique situation in making these ratings. Most leaders know enough about their own jobs and the jobs of their subordinates to do this.

To illustrate the effects of training and experience, let's examine the probe we just completed on the plant security chief. In this probe we described and rated the job of a security officer. The position came out as moderate in task structure (score = 11). Suppose, however, that we now know that the particular man in this position had very little training, perhaps a couple of short courses in security methods and procedures. We also know that he has been at this job for only four months, which is very little compared to other people in the field. His task structure rating scale would now look like the one on the following pages.

TASK STRUCTURE RATING SCALE — PART I

Circle the number in the appropriate column.	Usually True	Sometimes True	Seldom True
Is the Goal Clearly Stated or Known?			
1. Is there a blueprint, picture, model or detailed description available of the finished product or service?	2	1	(0)
2. Is there a person available to advise and give a description of the finished product or service, or how the job should be done?	(2)	1	0
Is There Only One Way to Accomplish the Task?			
3. Is there a step-by-step procedure, or a standard operating procedure which indicates in detail the process which is to be followed?	2	(1)	0
4. Is there a specific way to subdivide the task into separate parts or steps?	(2)	1	0
5. Are there some ways which are clearly recognized as better than others for performing this task?	(2)	1	0
Is There Only One Correct Answer or Solution?			
6. Is it obvious when the task is finished and the correct solution has been found?	2	(1)	0
7. Is there a book, manual, or job description which indicates the best solution or the best outcome for the task?	2	(1)	0
Is It Easy to Check Whether the Job Was Done Right?			
8. Is there a generally agreed understanding about the standards the particular product or service has to meet to be considered acceptable?	2	(1)	0
9. Is the evaluation of this task generally made on some quantitative basis?	2	1	(0)
10. Can the leader and the group find out how well the task has been accomplished in enough time to improve future performance?	2	(1)	0

SUBTOTAL ⟨ 11 ⟩

TASK STRUCTURE RATING SCALE — PART 2

Training and Experience Adjustment

NOTE: Do not adjust jobs with task structure scores of 6 or below.

(a) Compared to others in this or similar positions, how much *training* has the leader had?

3	②	1	0
No training at all	Very little training	A moderate amount of training	A great deal of training

(b) Compared to others in this or similar positions, how much *experience* has the leader had?

6	④	2	0
No experience at all	Very little experience	A moderate amount of experience	A great deal of experience

Add lines (a) and (b) of the training and experience adjustment, then *subtract* this from the subtotal given in Part 1.

Subtotal from Part 1. $\boxed{11}$

Subtract training and experience adjustment $\boxed{-6}$

Total Task Structure Score $\boxed{5}$

As you can see, this leadership position is now low in task structure because of the leader's lack of training and experience. Be sure, however, not to make a training and experience adjustment on situations in which the Part 1 score is lower than 6.

Complete the task structure scale on the following two pages for your *secondary leadership job.* You will use this score along with your LMR score later in the program to compute the combined situational control.

TASK STRUCTURE RATING SCALE — PART I

Circle the number in the appropriate column.	Usually True	Sometimes True	Seldom True
Is the Goal Clearly Stated or Known?			
1. Is there a blueprint, picture, model or detailed description available of the finished product or service?	2	(1)	0
2. Is there a person available to advise and give a description of the finished product or service, or how the job should be done?	(2)	1	0
Is There Only One Way to Accomplish the Task?			
3. Is there a step-by-step procedure, or a standard operating procedure which indicates in detail the process which is to be followed?	2	1	(0)
4. Is there a specific way to subdivide the task into separate parts or steps?	(2)	1	0
5. Are there some ways which are clearly recognized as better than others for performing this task?	(2)	1	0
Is There Only One Correct Answer or Solution?			
6. Is it obvious when the task is finished and the correct solution has been found?	(2)	1	0
7. Is there a book, manual, or job description which indicates the best solution or the best outcome for the task?	2	1	(0)
Is It Easy to Check Whether the Job Was Done Right?			
8. Is there a generally agreed understanding about the standards the particular product or service has to meet to be considered acceptable?	(2)	1	0
9. Is the evaluation of this task generally made on some quantitative basis?	2	1	(0)
10. Can the leader and the group find out how well the task has been accomplished in enough time to improve future performance?	(2)	1	0

7—13 moderate task

SUBTOTAL 13

TASK STRUCTURE RATING SCALE — PART 2

Training and Experience Adjustment

NOTE: Do not adjust jobs with task structure scores of 6 or below.

(a) Compared to others in this or similar positions, how much *training* has the leader had?

3	2	1	0
No training at all	Very little training	A moderate amount of training	A great deal of training

(b) Compared to others in this or similar positions, how much *experience* has the leader had?

6	4	2	0
No experience at all	Very little experience	A moderate amount of experience	A great deal of experience

Add lines (a) and (b) of the training and experience adjustment, then *subtract* this from the subtotal given in Part 1.

Subtotal from Part 1.

$\boxed{13}$

Subtract training and experience adjustment

$\boxed{-3}$

Total Task Structure Score

$\boxed{10}$

SUMMARY

Task structure means the degree to which procedures, goals, and evaluation of a task can be defined. The leader who is given a highly structured task enjoys considerably more influence and control than one who is given a very unstructured task. The structured task, typified by work done on an assembly line, by a blueprint, or a standard operating procedure, gives members of a work unit little reason or opportunity to challenge the leader's decisions, and it provides the leader with a great deal of assurance that the job can be accomplished as long as the task is done in accordance with specifications and the organization's procedures.

We measure task structure on the basis of four related questions:

1. Is the goal or outcome clearly stated or known?

2. Is there only one way to accomplish the task or are there innumerable methods which might be used to accomplish the goal?

3. Is there only one correct answer or solution, or many possible solutions to the problem or ways of performing the task?

4. Is it easy to check whether the job was done right, or is it difficult to evaluate the outcome of the task?

Training and experience tend to increase the structure of the task for the leader. Therefore, when we examine task structure we must take into account the amount of training and experience the leader has had.

CHAPTER SIX

Measuring Position Power

The final step in measuring situational control is to determine the amount of position power given to a leader. One obvious way in which an organization "gives" a leader power is by assigning him or her to a position which has certain rights, duties, and obligations. These usually include the use of rewards and punishments to enforce legitimate orders and directives. Let us take a closer look at the power which an organization vests in a position.

Leadership positions vary, of course, in how much formal power they confer on the occupant. In some cases, the leader can hire and fire at will, assign tasks or transfer a subordinate from one job to another, from one department to another, and even from one city to another. In some organizations the leader may only be allowed to give certain punishments. These may consist of official and unofficial reprimands, demotion, fines, or docking. They may also include giving pay raises, extra vacation days, time off, or more informally, giving a subordinate desirable job assignments. At the other extreme are leadership positions in which the leader has practically no official power to punish or reward. For instance, the chairperson of a volunteer committee can only try to persuade and cajole the other members or to praise them when they do a good job.

In between these two extremes, there is, of course, a wide range of position power. Most leadership positions give some power to punish and reward. Most leaders have the implicit right to praise or to give subordinates a "chewing out," to "lean on people," or to pat them on the back. Most positions permit the leader to assign tasks and to decide who will work with whom.

Remember, however, that power and authority are not simply "given" to the leader. No leader has absolute authority and all authority and power derives from the willingness of subordinates to accept the leader's right to lead. Not even in the military services, which give a great deal of formal position power to the legitimate leader, is the leader independent of subordinates.

There is truth in the old Army adage that "You can't make a man obey an order, but you can make him sorry that he didn't." But if too many people will not obey a leader's orders willingly, the leader will not keep the position long. Most leadership, if not all, is an implied social contract. Subordinates usually will do what they are asked because this will give them various rewards and satisfactions. When a leader behaves in an arbitrary manner, he is likely to lose the support of his subordinates. As a result, the system

MEASURING POSITION POWER   75

breaks down, the group dissolves, or the leader is replaced. Practically all leadership power is, therefore, exercised by common consent.

Problems arise when subordinates consider that regulations and rules are unreasonable or unfairly applied. This reaffirms that the leader's power and authority derive in large part from the consent and support of subordinates and that power and authority cannot simply be "given" to somebody in a leadership position.

Also important is the backing and support of leaders by their superiors. If leaders recommend a reward, an administrative change, or a particular punishment, and their recommendation is refused by their superior, then their power over their own subordinates is considerably lessened.

One of the things which makes leadership such a difficult job is the fine line which you, as the leader, must walk between maintaining your group members' support and the demands of the organization. The organization may demand more output but the employees may want to work at a more comfortable pace. It is your job to use your authority and position power to reach some acceptable compromise between the organization's demands and your subordinates' willingness to comply.

The position power rating scale consists of five questions about the power which the leader has at his or her disposal for directing the behavior of followers. You should be able to answer these questions from your knowledge of the kinds of privileges which the organization gives you. However, some questions require some judgment about the likely use of power or its effects in a particular situation. People generally tend to *underestimate* the power of their own position and overestimate the power of others. Most of us feel that we never have as much power as we need. Be sure to guard against that tendency in these ratings. Try your hand at the probes on the following pages. Remember to imagine yourself in the role of the leader in responding to these situations.

⟶ **PROBE 12**

Estimate the Position Power of a Captain of a naval vessel.

_____✓__ High

_____ Medium

_____ Low

Now rate this job on the Position Power Rating scale and compare your ratings with those provided in the feedback.

POSITION POWER RATING SCALE

Circle the number which best represents your answer.

1. Can the leader directly or by recommendation administer rewards and punishments to his subordinates?

(2)	1	0
Can act directly or can recommend with high effectiveness	Can recommend but with mixed results	No

2. Can the leader directly or by recommendation affect the promotion, demotion, hiring or firing of his subordinates?

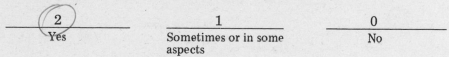

(2)	1	0
Can act directly or can recommend with high effectiveness	Can recommend but with mixed results	No

3. Does the leader have the knowledge necessary to assign tasks to subordinates and instruct them in task completion?

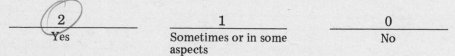

(2)	1	0
Yes	Sometimes or in some aspects	No

4. Is it the leader's job to evaluate the performance of his subordinates?

(2)	1	0
Yes	Sometimes or in some aspects	No

5. Has the leader been given some official title of authority by the organization (e.g., foreman, department head, platoon leader)?

(2)	0
Yes	No

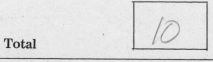

Total 10

FEEDBACK ⟵——————————————

POSITION POWER RATING SCALE

Circle the number which best represents your answer.

1. Can the leader directly or by recommendation administer rewards and punishments to his subordinates?

②	1	0
Can act directly or can recommend with high effectiveness	Can recommend but with mixed results	No

2. Can the leader directly or by recommendation affect the promotion, demotion, hiring or firing of his subordinates?

②	1	0
Can act directly or can recommend with high effectiveness	Can recommend but with mixed results	No

3. Does the leader have the knowledge necessary to assign tasks to subordinates and instruct them in task completion?

②	1	0
Yes	Sometimes or in some aspects	No

4. Is it the leader's job to evaluate the performance of his subordinates?

②	1	0
Yes	Sometimes or in some aspects	No

5. Has the leader been given some official title of authority by the organization (e.g., foreman, department head, platoon leader)?

②	0
Yes	No

Total   10

FEEDBACK ◄──────────────────────

This was an obvious probe. The captain of a ship has one of the most powerful positions that exists.

The position should have received the maximum number of points, 10. If you awarded this position anything over 7, you were still within range and should feel comfortable continuing on to the next probe. A score of 7-10 indicates *high* position power; a score of 4-6 shows moderate position power and a score of 3 or below denotes low position power.

The fact that position power is the least important of these three dimensions is reflected by comparing the total points possible on the scale to those obtained by completing the previous two scales. The highest score possible on position power is 10, the highest score on task structure is 20, and the highest leader-member relations score is 40.

If you missed this one, reread pages 74-75 before continuing.

PROBE 13

You have been appointed as the administrator of your company's research laboratory. You are assigned to coordinate and facilitate the research activities of a team of chemists, although you are not a chemist yourself.

In general, in this assignment you are supposed to furnish support for the research team's activities and to assure that important organizational and scientific procedures are followed. Your major responsibilities are to disburse already allocated funds, monitor progress toward goals, assign projects to available research teams, and supervise the nonresearch aspects of the laboratory (e.g., proper invoice procedures, report filing, use of equipment).

You are occasionally asked to report on individual team members, but your reports make up only a part of the members' overall evaluation. Your recommendations are not weighted very strongly; the major evaluations are made by the team leaders who direct the work of the team. Since you have many other responsibilities, you are not asked to evaluate the scientific work of the group.

Your position power is likely to be:

_____ High

_____ Moderate

___✓___ Low

Now rate this job on the Position Power Rating scale and compare your ratings with those provided in the feedback.

POSITION POWER RATING SCALE

Circle the number which best represents your answer.

1. Can the leader directly or by recommendation administer rewards and punishments to his subordinates?

2	1	0
Can act directly or can recommend with high effectiveness	Can recommend but with mixed results	No

2. Can the leader directly or by recommendation affect the promotion, demotion, hiring or firing of his subordinates?

2	1	0
Can act directly or can recommend with high effectiveness	Can recommend but with mixed results	No

3. Does the leader have the knowledge necessary to assign tasks to subordinates and instruct them in task completion?

2	1	0
Yes	Sometimes or in some aspects	No

4. Is it the leader's job to evaluate the performance of his subordinates?

2	1	0
Yes	Sometimes or in some aspects	No

5. Has the leader been given some official title of authority by the organization (e.g., foreman, department head, platoon leader)?

2	0
Yes	No

Total   5

FEEDBACK ←————————————————

POSITION POWER RATING SCALE

Circle the number which best represents your answer.

1. Can the leader directly or by recommendation administer rewards and punishments to his subordinates?

2	1	⓪
Can act directly or can recommend with high effectiveness	Can recommend but with mixed results	No

2. Can the leader directly or by recommendation affect the promotion, demotion, hiring or firing of his subordinates?

2	1	⓪
Can act directly or can recommend with high effectiveness	Can recommend but with mixed results	No

3. Does the leader have the knowledge necessary to assign tasks to subordinates and instruct them in task completion?

2	①	0
Yes	Sometimes or in some aspects	No

4. Is it the leader's job to evaluate the performance of his subordinates?

2	①	0
Yes	Sometimes or in some aspects	No

5. Has the leader been given some official title of authority by the organization (e.g., foreman, department head, platoon leader)?

②	0
Yes	No

Total   4

FEEDBACK ◄─────────────────────────

This position is moderate in terms of power. The administrator does have
certain areas of authority and an official position. However, lack of expertise
(and consequently, responsibility) keeps the administrator from having much
of an impact on the work of the team members.

The leader does, however, have an official title so score 2 points for
question 5, occasionally evaluates team member performance as *part* of an
overall evaluation, and makes job assignments. Therefore, questions 3 and 4
should be given a score of 1.

A total score of 4 is appropriate. If you had trouble with this probe,
review pages 74-75 before continuing.

⸻⸻⸻⸻⸻⸻⸻⸻⸻⸻⸻⸻➤   **PROBE 14**

You are the assistant production manager in a paper products corporation. A
scuffle has occurred in the sealing assembly line and one man has broken his
wrist. The Director of Production wishes to undertake an investigation immediately. He has appointed a board of inquiry of three supervisors and a union
official to look into the matter. Because of your position, you have been
asked to chair this unofficial inquiry. You have eight hours to file a report.
　　Your position power is:

_____ High

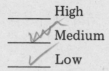_____ Medium

_____ Low

Now rate the job on the position rating scale.

POSITION POWER RATING SCALE

Circle the number which best represents your answer.

1. Can the leader directly or by recommendation administer rewards and punishments to his subordinates?

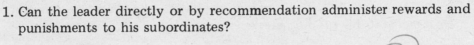

2	1	0
Can act directly or can recommend with high effectiveness	Can recommend but with mixed results	No

2. Can the leader directly or by recommendation affect the promotion, demotion, hiring or firing of his subordinates?

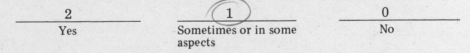

2	1	0
Can act directly or can recommend with high effectiveness	Can recommend but with mixed results	No

3. Does the leader have the knowledge necessary to assign tasks to subordinates and instruct them in task completion?

2	1	0
Yes	Sometimes or in some aspects	No

4. Is it the leader's job to evaluate the performance of his subordinates?

2	1	0
Yes	Sometimes or in some aspects	No

5. Has the leader been given some official title of authority by the organization (e.g., foreman, department head, platoon leader)?

2	0
Yes	No

Total   3

FEEDBACK ◄───────────────────────►

POSITION POWER RATING SCALE

Circle the number which best represents your answer.

1. Can the leader directly or by recommendation administer rewards and punishments to his subordinates?

2	1	⓪
Can act directly or can recommend with high effectiveness	Can recommend but with mixed results	No

2. Can the leader directly or by recommendation affect the promotion, demotion, hiring or firing of his subordinates?

2	1	⓪
Can act directly or can recommend with high effectiveness	Can recommend but with mixed results	No

3. Does the leader have the knowledge necessary to assign tasks to subordinates and instruct them in task completion?

2	①	0
Yes	Sometimes or in some aspects	No

4. Is it the leader's job to evaluate the performance of his subordinates?

2	1	⓪
Yes	Sometimes or in some aspects	No

5. Has the leader been given some official title of authority by the organization (e.g., foreman, department head, platoon leader)?

②	0
Yes	No

Total   3

FEEDBACK ◄───────────────────────

This position clearly has low position power, a score of 3. It is a short term committee, with no official sanction. Of course, most important is the fact that you will be chairing a *committee*. This drastically reduces your power over your subordinates, namely, *the other members of this board.* You will not be expected to punish or reward your fellow board members.

If you are having difficulty with the position power scale, be sure and review the chapter.

Now that you have had some experience with the position power scale, complete the scale on the following page for your *secondary leadership job*, by circling the answer which best represents how you see the job. Then add the numbers of your choices, and enter the total at the bottom of the page.

Remember that a score of 7-10 indicates high position power; a score of 4-6 shows you have moderate position power, and a score of 3 or below denotes low position power. We will use this score in the next chapter.

POSITION POWER RATING SCALE

Circle the number which best represents your answer.

1. Can the leader directly or by recommendation administer rewards and punishments to his subordinates?

2	(1)	0
Can act directly or can recommend with high effectiveness	Can recommend but with mixed results	No

2. Can the leader directly or by recommendation affect the promotion, demotion, hiring or firing of his subordinates?

2	(1)	0
Can act directly or can recommend with high effectiveness	Can recommend but with mixed results	No

3. Does the leader have the knowledge necessary to assign tasks to subordinates and instruct them in task completion?

(2)	1	0
Yes	Sometimes or in some aspects	No

4. Is it the leader's job to evaluate the performance of his subordinates?

2	(1)	0
Yes	Sometimes or in some aspects	No

5. Has the leader been given some official title of authority by the organization (e.g., foreman, department head, platoon leader)?

(2)	0
Yes	No

Total   7

SUMMARY

Position power means the authority and control which a person has by virtue of occupying a particular leadership position. It includes the means leaders have at their disposal for assuring that their legitimate orders and directives are carried out. These include such methods of punishment as reprimanding, scolding, docking, demoting, or, in the last resort, firing a subordinate. They may include such rewards as promotion, raises, praise, or recommending raises or promotions, as well as giving desirable assignments.

While power officially is conferred by the organization, the power of leaders is derived from their subordinates' willingness to accept the leader's authority.

The power of leaders is also affected by their knowledge of the job and their ability to assign tasks.

Finally, the power of leaders is affected by the support they get from their superiors. If their recommendations are generally followed, then their power will appear greater in the eyes of subordinates.

A leader's power is affected by the support he gets from his boss.

CHAPTER SEVEN

Computing Situational Control

The previous chapters introduced the three major factors which affect the leader's control of a situation and provided practice in diagnosing and rating various jobs. These factors are leader-member relations; task structure, training, and experience; and position power. The combined situational control score is derived by simply adding the scores for the three scales. Your score will fall into either the high control, moderate control, or low control area. How these dimensions are combined to form the three zones is illustrated below:

	High Control	Moderate Control		Low Control
Leader-Member Relations	Good	Good	Poor	Poor
Task Structure	High	Low } or {	High	Low
Position Power	High	Low	High	Low

On the following page is the scale used to combine the three dimensions into the overall situational control rating. To complete this rating for your *secondary leadership job*, transfer your scores from each of the three scales you completed earlier. First enter your leader-member relations score from page 46. The task structure scale completed for your secondary job can be found on page 72. Finally, enter your position power total from page 89.

Add the figures in each of the three boxes to determine your total situational control score. The score on the table at the bottom of the page gives you the amount of situational control for this secondary job. Be sure to check your addition!

Does this score seem right in light of your experience? If not, review the various scales. Were you too strict or too lenient with yourself? Did you misunderstand the scoring procedure? Can it be that you misread the situational control of your secondary leadership job?

After you have completed computing your situational control for your secondary leadership job, complete the probes on the following pages. Remember to respond as the leader of each group described.

SITUATIONAL CONTROL SCALE

Enter the total scores for the Leader-Member Relations dimension, the Task Structure scale, and the Position Power scale in the spaces below. Add the three scores together and compare your total with the ranges given in the table below to determine your overall situational control.

1. *Leader-Member Relations Total* $\boxed{25}$

2. *Task Structure Total* $\boxed{10}$

3. *Position Power Total* $\boxed{7}$

Grand Total $\boxed{42}$

Total Score	51 - 70	31 - 50	10 - 30
Amount of Situational Control	High Control	Moderate Control	Low Control

---

→ **PROBE 15**

A dog food company is looking for a person to supervise their shipping docks and you have decided to apply for the job. The shipping supervisor keeps track of invoices and fills and ships orders. He or she directs the work of various clerks and stockhandlers to see that orders are promptly filled and shipped to the customers; and the supervisor is also responsible for making sure that incoming raw material is properly received and routed to the right departments.

The company is doing well and morale is good. This work group has been together for a long time and has always worked well together. There has been little evidence of dissension. In fact, the members have organized a bowling team and have been playing one night a week, and their families occasionally socialize.

Relations with management have been traditionally excellent in this department. Prior to starting the job, you will be given an intensive training course in the company's shipping procedures, although you feel you have had adequate experience in a shipping department in a previous nonsupervisory job.

The shipping and receiving procedures are highly standardized as is the paper work. The shipping supervisor is a first level manager with the same rank as that of a foreman. As such, the supervisor is expected to maintain discipline and company standards, make job assignments, and evaluate employee performance at regular intervals. While the supervisor does not hire and fire, his or her recommendations are given considerable weight.

What is your estimate of situational control for this job?

_____✓ High Control

_____ Moderate Control

_____ Low Control

On the following pages complete the leader-member relations, task structure, and position power scales for the shipping supervisor's position. Then rate the situational control and compare these ratings with the estimate you made above. Look at the feedback and see how close you came to the ratings we provided.

LEADER-MEMBER RELATIONS SCALE

Circle the number which best represents your response to each item.

	strongly agree	agree	neither agree nor disagree	disagree	strongly disagree
1. The people I supervise have trouble getting along with each other.	1	2	3	4	(5)
2. My subordinates are reliable and trustworthy.	(5)	4	3	2	1
3. There seems to be a friendly atmosphere among the people I supervise.	(5)	4	3	2	1
4. My subordinates always cooperate with me in getting the job done.	5	4	(3)	2	1
5. There is friction between my subordinates and myself.	1	2	3	4	(5)
6. My subordinates give me a good deal of help and support in getting the job done.	5	(4)	3	2	1
7. The people I supervise work well together in getting the job done.	(5)	4	3	2	1
8. I have good relations with the people I supervise.	5	4	(3)	2	1

Total Score 35

TASK STRUCTURE RATING SCALE — PART I

Circle the number in the appropriate column.	Usually True	Sometimes True	Seldom True
Is the Goal Clearly Stated or Known?			
1. Is there a blueprint, picture, model or detailed description available of the finished product or service?	(2)	1	0
2. Is there a person available to advise and give a description of the finished product or service, or how the job should be done?	2	1 ←	(0)
Is There Only One Way to Accomplish the Task?			
3. Is there a step-by-step procedure, or a standard operating procedure which indicates in detail the process which is to be followed?	(2)	1	0
4. Is there a specific way to subdivide the task into separate parts or steps?	(2)	1	0
5. Are there some ways which are clearly recognized as better than others for performing this task?	2	(1)	0
Is There Only One Correct Answer or Solution?			
6. Is it obvious when the task is finished and the correct solution has been found?	(2)	1	0
7. Is there a book, manual, or job description which indicates the best solution or the best outcome for the task?	2	1	(0)
Is It Easy to Check Whether the Job Was Done Right?			
8. Is there a generally agreed understanding about the standards the particular product or service has to meet to be considered acceptable?	(2)	1	0
9. Is the evaluation of this task generally made on some quantitative basis?	2	1	(0)
10. Can the leader and the group find out how well the task has been accomplished in enough time to improve future performance?	(2)	1	0

SUBTOTAL   13

TASK STRUCTURE RATING SCALE — PART 2

Training and Experience Adjustment

NOTE: Do not adjust jobs with task structure scores of 6 or below.

(a) Compared to others in this or similar positions, how much *training* has the leader had?

3	2	①1	0
No training at all	Very little training	A moderate amount of training	A great deal of training

(b) Compared to others in this or similar positions, how much *experience* has the leader had?

6	4	②2	0
No experience at all	Very little experience	A moderate amount of experience	A great deal of experience

Add lines (a) and (b) of the training and experience adjustment, then *subtract* this from the subtotal given in Part 1.

Subtotal from Part 1. | 13 |

Subtract training and experience adjustment | −3 |

Total Task Structure Score | 10 |

POSITION POWER RATING SCALE

Circle the number which best represents your answer.

1. Can the leader directly or by recommendation administer rewards and punishments to his subordinates?

2	1	0
Can act directly or can recommend with high effectiveness	Can recommend but with mixed results	No

2. Can the leader directly or by recommendation affect the promotion, demotion, hiring or firing of his subordinates?

2	1	0
Can act directly or can recommend with high effectiveness	Can recommend but with mixed results	No

3. Does the leader have the knowledge necessary to assign tasks to subordinates and instruct them in task completion?

2	1	0
Yes	Sometimes or in some aspects	No

4. Is it the leader's job to evaluate the performance of his subordinates?

2	1	0
Yes	Sometimes or in some aspects	No

5. Has the leader been given some official title of authority by the organization (e.g., foreman, department head, platoon leader)?

2	0
Yes	No

Total   10

SITUATIONAL CONTROL SCALE

Enter the total scores for the Leader-Member Relations dimension, the Task Structure scale, and the Position Power scale in the spaces below. Add the three scores together and compare your total with the ranges given in the table below to determine your overall situational control.

1. *Leader-Member Relations Total*   `35`

2. *Task Structure Total*   `10`

3. *Position Power Total*   `10`

Grand Total   `55`

Total Score	51 - 70	31 - 50	10 - 30
Amount of Situational Control	High Control	Moderate Control	Low Control

FEEDBACK ←—————————————————————

LEADER-MEMBER RELATIONS SCALE

Circle the number which best represents your response to each item.

	strongly agree	agree	neither agree nor disagree	disagree	strongly disagree
1. The people I supervise have trouble getting along with each other.	1	2	3	4	(5)
2. My subordinates are reliable and trustworthy.	(5)	4	3	2	1
3. There seems to be a friendly atmosphere among the people I supervise.	(5)	4	3	2	1
4. My subordinates always cooperate with me in getting the job done.	5	4	(3)	2	1
5. There is friction between my subordinates and myself.	1	2	(3)	4	5
6. My subordinates give me a good deal of help and support in getting the job done.	5	4	(3)	2	1
7. The people I supervise work well together in getting the job done.	(5)	4	3	2	1
8. I have good relations with the people I supervise.	5	4	(3)	2	1

Total Score $\boxed{32}$

FEEDBACK ←─────────────────────────────

TASK STRUCTURE RATING SCALE — PART I

Circle the number in the appropriate column.	Usually True	Sometimes True	Seldom True

Is the Goal Clearly Stated or Known?

1. Is there a blueprint, picture, model or detailed description available of the finished product or service? — (2) 1 0

2. Is there a person available to advise and give a description of the finished product or service, or how the job should be done? — 2 (1) 0

Is There Only One Way to Accomplish the Task?

3. Is there a step-by-step procedure, or a standard operating procedure which indicates in detail the process which is to be followed? — (2) 1 0

4. Is there a specific way to subdivide the task into separate parts or steps? — (2) 1 0

5. Are there some ways which are clearly recognized as better than others for performing this task? — (2) 1 0

Is There Only One Correct Answer or Solution?

6. Is is obvious when the task is finished and the correct solution has been found? — (2) 1 0

7. Is there a book, manual, or job description which indicates the best solution or the best outcome for the task? — 2 (1) 0

Is It Easy to Check Whether the Job Was Done Right?

8. Is there a generally agreed understanding about the standards the particular product or service has to meet to be considered acceptable? — (2) 1 0

9. Is the evaluation of this task generally made on some quantitative basis? — 2 (1) 0

10. Can the leader and the group find out how well the task has been accomplished in enough time to improve future performance? — (2) 1 0

SUBTOTAL | *17* |

FEEDBACK ◄───────────────────────────

TASK STRUCTURE RATING SCALE — PART 2

Training and Experience Adjustment

Note: **Do not adjust jobs with task structure scores of 6 or below.**

(a) Compared to others in this or similar positions, how much *training* has the leader had?

3	2	1	(0)
No training at all	Very little training	A moderate amount of training	A great deal of training

(b) Compared to others in this or similar positions, how much *experience* has the leader had?

6	4	(2)	0
No experience at all	Very little experience	A moderate amount of experience	A great deal of experience

Add lines (a) and (b) of the training and experience adjustment, then *subtract* this from the subtotal given in Part 1.

Subtotal from Part 1. | 17 |

Subtract training and experience adjustment | -2 |

Total Task Structure Score | 15 |

FEEDBACK ←————————————————→

POSITION POWER RATING SCALE

Circle the number which best represents your answer.

1. Can the leader directly or by recommendation administer rewards and punishments to his subordinates?

②	1	0
Can act directly or can recommend with high effectiveness	Can recommend but with mixed results	No

2. Can the leader directly or by recommendation affect the promotion, demotion, hiring or firing of his subordinates?

②	1	0
Can act directly or can recommend with high effectiveness	Can recommend but with mixed results	No

3. Does the leader have the knowledge necessary to assign tasks to subordinates and instruct them in task completion?

②	1	0
Yes	Sometimes or in some aspects	No

4. Is it the leader's job to evaluate the performance of his subordinates?

②	1	0
Yes	Sometimes or in some aspects	No

5. Has the leader been given some official title of authority by the organization (e.g., foreman, department head, platoon leader)?

②	0
Yes	No

Total | 10 |

FEEDBACK ◄─────────────────────────

SITUATIONAL CONTROL SCALE

Enter the total scores for the Leader-Member Relations dimension, the Task Structure scale, and the Position Power scale in the spaces below. Add the three scores together and compare your total with the ranges given in the table below to determine your overall situational control.

1. *Leader-Member Relations Total*

$$\boxed{32}$$

2. *Task Structure Total*

$$\boxed{15}$$

3. *Position Power Total*

$$\boxed{10}$$

Grand Total

$$\boxed{57}$$

Total Score	51 - 70	31 - 50	10 - 30
Amount of Situational Control	High Control	Moderate Control	Low Control

FEEDBACK ←────────────────────────

As the short description indicated to you, morale and *leader-member relations* in the company are generally very good, and there is no reason to expect that the shipping supervisor will have any difficulties. A score of 32 would be appropriate on the LMR scale; however, a score of 30 or above would be acceptable. You will notice that we have scored questions 4, 5, 6, and 8 as neither agree nor disagree. This was done because we do not know for sure how the new shipping manager will get along with the subordinates in the department. We have no reason to believe their relationship will be poor nor do we know it will be exceptionally good. The best strategy in this case is to select the middle answer, neither agree nor disagree. The rest of the questions, however, should receive the maximum points since we do know the group members get along well with each other.

Task structure is, of course, quite high for this job. Note that the shipping manager is not required to innovate in managing shipping docks, completing the paperwork, and seeing that goods are properly routed. We rated all questions except 2, 7, and 9 on the task structure scales as "usually." Question 2 received a "sometimes" since the manager probably does not have someone available to advise at all times. Question 7 was scored "sometimes" since the shipping dock job would not have a written manual providing *all* the best solutions or outcomes. Obviously, the manager will have to make some decisions on his or her own. Question 9 received a "sometimes" since there is little quantitative evaluation made of the shipping procedures. This provided us with a subtotal of 17. Because the manager would receive an extensive training program, there was no training adjustment. However, because the manager's experience was "adequate" in a nonsupervisory job, we subtracted two points from the total score. The task structure score was 15. If your score was above 14, you understood the problem well.

The *position power* is that of a line manager and quite high. You could safely have answered with the maximum points for all questions. However, if your score is above 7, you are in the right range.

This would give you a total situational control score of 57: a situation of *high control*. If your score was over 50, you did well and should move on to the next probe. If you missed this one, carefully compare your scales to the feedback to determine where you made your mistake.

→ PROBE 16

You are the assistant to the Director of Employee Relations for a large (8,000 employee) manufacturing company. The morale of the firm is quite good; profits are up and, by and large, the workers are satisfied. The company has decided to organize an extensive recreational program available to all employees and a committee is being set up to study the question.

You have been selected to chair the committee. You have been allowed to choose your own committee so interpersonal relations should be excellent. As chairperson, you will have no official power, but will simply coordinate and guide the work of the committee.

What is your estimate of situational control for this job?

_____ High Control

_____ Moderate Control

___✓___ Low Control

On the following pages rate the situational control for this job and compare these ratings with the estimate you have made. Then look at the feedback and see how close you came to the ratings we provided.

LEADER-MEMBER RELATIONS SCALE

Circle the number which best represents your response to each item.

	strongly agree	agree	neither agree nor disagree	disagree	strongly disagree
1. The people I supervise have trouble getting along with each other.	1	2	3	(4)	5
2. My subordinates are reliable and trustworthy.	5	(4)	3	2	1
3. There seems to be a friendly atmosphere among the people I supervise.	(5)	4	3	2	1
4. My subordinates always cooperate with me in getting the job done.	5	4	(3)	2	1
5. There is friction between my subordinates and myself.	1	2	3	4	(5)
6. My subordinates give me a good deal of help and support in getting the job done.	5	4	(3)	2	1
7. The people I supervise work well together in getting the job done.	5	(4)	3	2	1
8. I have good relations with the people I supervise.	(5)	4	3	2	1

Total Score

TASK STRUCTURE RATING SCALE — PART I

Circle the number in the appropriate column.	Usually True	Sometimes True	Seldom True

Is the Goal Clearly Stated or Known?

1. Is there a blueprint, picture, model or detailed description available of the finished product or service? — 2 — 1 — (0)

2. Is there a person available to advise and give a description of the finished product or service, or how the job should be done? — 2 — 1 — (0)

Is There Only One Way to Accomplish the Task?

3. Is there a step-by-step procedure, or a standard operating procedure which indicates in detail the process which is to be followed? — 2 — 1 — (0)

4. Is there a specific way to subdivide the task into separate parts or steps? — 2 — 1 — (0)

5. Are there some ways which are clearly recognized as better than others for performing this task? — 2 — 1 — (0)

Is There Only One Correct Answer or Solution?

6. Is it obvious when the task is finished and the correct solution has been found? — 2 — (1) — 0

7. Is there a book, manual, or job description which indicates the best solution or the best outcome for the task? — 2 — 1 — (0)

Is It Easy to Check Whether the Job Was Done Right?

8. Is there a generally agreed understanding about the standards the particular product or service has to meet to be considered acceptable? — 2 — (1) — 0

9. Is the evaluation of this task generally made on some quantitative basis? — 2 — 1 — (0)

10. Can the leader and the group find out how well the task has been accomplished in enough time to improve future performance? — 2 — 1 — (0)

SUBTOTAL [2]

TASK STRUCTURE RATING SCALE — PART 2

Training and Experience Adjustment

NOTE: Do not adjust jobs with task structure scores of 6 or below.

(a)   Compared to others in this or similar positions, how much *training* has the leader had?

3	2	1	0
No training at all	Very little training	A moderate amount of training	A great deal of training

(b)   Compared to others in this or similar positions, how much *experience* has the leader had?

6	4	2	0
No experience at all	Very little experience	A moderate amount of experience	A great deal of experience

Add lines (a) and (b) of the training and experience adjustment, then *subtract* this from the subtotal given in Part 1.

Subtotal from Part 1.   2

Subtract training and experience adjustment   —

Total Task Structure Score

POSITION POWER RATING SCALE

Circle the number which best represents your answer.

1. Can the leader directly or by recommendation administer rewards and punishments to his subordinates?

2	1	0
Can act directly or can recommend with high effectiveness	Can recommend but with mixed results	No

2. Can the leader directly or by recommendation affect the promotion, demotion, hiring or firing of his subordinates?

2	1	0
Can act directly or can recommend with high effectiveness	Can recommend but with mixed results	No

3. Does the leader have the knowledge necessary to assign tasks to subordinates and instruct them in task completion?

2	1	0
Yes	Sometimes or in some aspects	No

4. Is it the leader's job to evaluate the performance of his subordinates?

2	1	0
Yes	Sometimes or in some aspects	No

5. Has the leader been given some official title of authority by the organization (e.g., foreman, department head, platoon leader)?

2	0
Yes	No

Total   4

SITUATIONAL CONTROL SCALE

Enter the total scores for the Leader-Member Relations dimension, the Task Structure scale, and the Position Power scale in the spaces below. Add the three scores together and compare your total with the ranges given in the table below to determine your overall situational control.

1. *Leader-Member Relations Total*   33

2. *Task Structure Total*   0

3. *Position Power Total*   4

Grand Total   39

Total Score	51 - 70	31 - 50	10 - 30
Amount of Situational Control	High Control	Moderate Control	Low Control

FEEDBACK ←————————————

LEADER-MEMBER RELATIONS SCALE

Circle the number which best represents your response to each item.

	strongly agree	agree	neither agree nor disagree	disagree	strongly disagree
1. The people I supervise have trouble getting along with each other.	1	2	3	4	(5)
2. My subordinates are reliable and trustworthy.	(5)	4	3	2	1
3. There seems to be a friendly atmosphere among the people I supervise.	(5)	4	3	2	1
4. My subordinates always cooperate with me in getting the job done.	(5)	4	3	2	1
5. There is friction between my subordinates and myself.	1	2	3	4	(5)
6. My subordinates give me a good deal of help and support in getting the job done.	(5)	4	3	2	1
7. The people I supervise work well together in getting the job done.	(5)	4	3	2	1
8. I have good relations with the people I supervise.	(5)	4	3	2	1

Total Score ⟨ 40 ⟩

FEEDBACK ◄─────────────────────

TASK STRUCTURE RATING SCALE — PART I

Circle the number in the appropriate column.	Usually True	Sometimes True	Seldom True
Is the Goal Clearly Stated or Known?			
1. Is there a blueprint, picture, model or detailed description available of the finished product or service?	2	1	**(0)**
2. Is there a person available to advise and give a description of the finished product or service, or how the job should be done?	2	1	**(0)**
Is There Only One Way to Accomplish the Task?			
3. Is there a step-by-step procedure, or a standard operating procedure which indicates in detail the process which is to be followed?	2	1	**(0)**
4. Is there a specific way to subdivide the task into separate parts or steps?	2	1	**(0)**
5. Are there some ways which are clearly recognized as better than others for performing this task?	2	**(1)**	0
Is There Only One Correct Answer or Solution?			
6. Is is obvious when the task is finished and the correct solution has been found?	2	1	**(0)**
7. Is there a book, manual, or job description which indicates the best solution or the best outcome for the task?	2	1	**(0)**
Is It Easy to Check Whether the Job Was Done Right?			
8. Is there a generally agreed understanding about the standards the particular product or service has to meet to be considered acceptable?	2	1	**(0)**
9. Is the evaluation of this task generally made on some quantitative basis?	2	**(1)**	0
10. Can the leader and the group find out how well the task has been accomplished in enough time to improve future performance?	2	**(1)**	0

SUBTOTAL   **3**

FEEDBACK ◄────────────────────────

TASK STRUCTURE RATING SCALE — PART 2

Training and Experience Adjustment

Note: Do not adjust jobs with task structure scores of 6 or below.

(a) Compared to others in this or similar positions, how much *training* has the leader had?

$\underline{\hspace{1em}3\hspace{1em}}$	$\underline{\hspace{1em}2\hspace{1em}}$	$\underline{\hspace{2em}1\hspace{2em}}$	$\underline{\hspace{2em}0\hspace{2em}}$
No training at all	Very little training	A moderate amount of training	A great deal of training

(b) Compared to others in this or similar positions, how much *experience* has the leader had?

$\underline{\hspace{1em}6\hspace{1em}}$	$\underline{\hspace{1em}4\hspace{1em}}$	$\underline{\hspace{2em}2\hspace{2em}}$	$\underline{\hspace{2em}0\hspace{2em}}$
No experience at all	Very little experience	A moderate amount of experience	A great deal of experience

Add lines (a) and (b) of the training and experience adjustment, then *subtract* this from the subtotal given in Part 1.

Subtotal from Part 1.   **3**

Subtract training and experience adjustment   **—** *

Total Task Structure Score   **3**

*No adjustment necessary since Part 1 score is less than 6.

FEEDBACK ◄─────────────────────────

POSITION POWER RATING SCALE

Circle the number which best represents your answer.

1. Can the leader directly or by recommendation administer rewards and punishments to his subordinates?

2	1	(0)
Can act directly or can recommend with high effectiveness	Can recommend but with mixed results	No

2. Can the leader directly or by recommendation affect the promotion, demotion, hiring or firing of his subordinates?

2	1	(0)
Can act directly or can recommend with high effectiveness	Can recommend but with mixed results	No

3. Does the leader have the knowledge necessary to assign tasks to subordinates and instruct them in task completion?

2	1	(0)
Yes	Sometimes or in some aspects	No

4. Is it the leader's job to evaluate the performance of his subordinates?

2	1	(0)
Yes	Sometimes or in some aspects	No

5. Has the leader been given some official title of authority by the organization (e.g., foreman, department head, platoon leader)?

(2)	0
Yes	No

Total | 2 |

FEEDBACK ◄─────────────────────────

SITUATIONAL CONTROL SCALE

Enter the total scores for the Leader-Member Relations dimension, the Task Structure scale, and the Position Power scale in the spaces below. Add the three scores together and compare your total with the ranges given in the table below to determine your overall situational control.

1. *Leader-Member Relations Total*

$$40$$

2. *Task Structure Total*

$$3$$

3. *Position Power Total*

$$2$$

Grand Total

$$45$$

Total Score	51 - 70	31 - 50	10 - 30
Amount of Situational Control	High Control	Moderate Control	Low Control

FEEDBACK ←————————————————————————

You are, of course, told that the *leader-member relations* are quite good. But even if you had not been given this information, the chances are that a job like this, to chair a committee which will organize a recreational program, is not likely to create too much tension. A score of 25-40 would be appropriate.

The *task* here would be *highly unstructured*. To be sure, the committee is to propose a recreational program, but the nature of the program, its organization, and the details for its implementation are all left open. On the task structure rating scale all items except 5, 9, and 10 received "seldom" thereby accumulating zero points. Question 5 was answered "sometimes" since there would be some ways that are better than others for organizing the task. Questions 9 and 10 also scored 1 point each since there would be some opportunity as you progress on the project to get feedback on whether the recreational program is adequate. Because the total score is so low, no training and experience adjustment is required. A score of 3 is about right.

As in almost all of these kinds of situations, the chairperson of such a committee will have very *low position power*. About the only place this job would score on the position power scale would be question 5 — the chairperson does have an official title. This would be worth 2 points.

Basically, the relations between the chairperson and members will be good, and the task will be unstructured, having low position power. This situation, therefore, would be moderate in control. A score between 31 and 50 would be appropriate.

If you got this one right, you are on the way to being an expert. Keep up the good work.

---------------------------------→ **PROBE 17**

You have been selected as the director of a laboratory for research and development of a large plastics firm. Your predecessor was fired for maintaining sloppy financial records and accounting procedures, and for poor management of the laboratory's program. The rest of the laboratory research staff is quite upset and several have considered quitting. Much hostility exists between the research staff and management. Although complete information on the situation is not available, the leader-member relations with the acting-director are quite strained. In fact, this interim director filled out a leader-member relations scale for you and came up with a score of 16.

You have been working in another laboratory on the West Coast and feel you have average experience and training for the job. As before, you will supervise the research staff and be responsible for evaluating the staff and recommending changes. These recommendations are given consideration by upper management along with other available information.

As in practically all research efforts, there is no way to specify exactly how the work is to be done and what procedures are to be followed in seeking new products or in developing new programs. The expectation is, however, that the laboratory will come up with marketable products which will benefit the company.

What is your estimate of the situational control for this job?

_____ High Control

_____ Moderate Control

_____ Low Control

On the following pages rate the situational control for the job and compare these ratings with the estimate you have made. Then look at the feedback, and see how close you came to the ratings we provided.

LEADER-MEMBER RELATIONS SCALE

Circle the number which best represents your response to each item.

	strongly agree	agree	neither agree nor disagree	disagree	strongly disagree
1. The people I supervise have trouble getting along with each other.	1	2	③	4	5
2. My subordinates are reliable and trustworthy.	5	4	3	②	1
3. There seems to be a friendly atmosphere among the people I supervise.	5	4	3	②	1
4. My subordinates always cooperate with me in getting the job done.	5	4	③	2	1
5. There is friction between my subordinates and myself.	①	2	3	4	5
6. My subordinates give me a good deal of help and support in getting the job done.	5	4	3	②	1
7. The people I supervise work well together in getting the job done.	5	4	3	2	①
8. I have good relations with the people I supervise.	5	4	3	②	1

Total Score *16*

*according to the
interim director's
LMR rating

TASK STRUCTURE RATING SCALE — PART I

Circle the number in the appropriate column.	Usually True	Sometimes True	Seldom True

Is the Goal Clearly Stated or Known?

1. Is there a blueprint, picture, model or detailed description available of the finished product or service? — 2, 1, (0)

2. Is there a person available to advise and give a description of the finished product or service, or how the job should be done? — 2, 1, (0)

Is There Only One Way to Accomplish the Task?

3. Is there a step-by-step procedure, or a standard operating procedure which indicates in detail the process which is to be followed? — 2, (1), 0

4. Is there a specific way to subdivide the task into separate parts or steps? — 2, 1, (0)

5. Are there some ways which are clearly recognized as better than others for performing this task? — 2, (1), 0

Is There Only One Correct Answer or Solution?

6. Is it obvious when the task is finished and the correct solution has been found? — 2, (1), 0

7. Is there a book, manual, or job description which indicates the best solution or the best outcome for the task? — 2, 1, (0)

Is It Easy to Check Whether the Job Was Done Right?

8. Is there a generally agreed understanding about the standards the particular product or service has to meet to be considered acceptable? — 2, (1), 0

9. Is the evaluation of this task generally made on some quantitative basis? — 2, (1), 0

10. Can the leader and the group find out how well the task has been accomplished in enough time to improve future performance? — 2, 1, (0)

SUBTOTAL [5]

TASK STRUCTURE RATING SCALE — PART 2

Training and Experience Adjustment

NOTE: Do not adjust jobs with task structure scores of 6 or below.

(a) Compared to others in this or similar positions, how much *training* has the leader had?

3	2	1	0
No training at all	Very little training	A moderate amount of training	A great deal of training

(b) Compared to others in this or similar positions, how much *experience* has the leader had?

6	4	2	0
No experience at all	Very little experience	A moderate amount of experience	A great deal of experience

Add lines (a) and (b) of the training and experience adjustment, then *subtract* this from the subtotal given in Part 1.

Subtotal from Part 1.

Subtract training and experience adjustment

Total Task Structure Score   5

POSITION POWER RATING SCALE

Circle the number which best represents your answer.

1. Can the leader directly or by recommendation administer rewards and punishments to his subordinates?

2	(1)	0
Can act directly or can recommend with high effectiveness	Can recommend but with mixed results	No

2. Can the leader directly or by recommendation affect the promotion, demotion, hiring or firing of his subordinates?

2	(1)	0
Can act directly or can recommend with high effectiveness	Can recommend but with mixed results	No

3. Does the leader have the knowledge necessary to assign tasks to subordinates and instruct them in task completion?

2	(1)	0
Yes	Sometimes or in some aspects	No

4. Is it the leader's job to evaluate the performance of his subordinates?

(2)	1	0
Yes	Sometimes or in some aspects	No

5. Has the leader been given some official title of authority by the organization (e.g., foreman, department head, platoon leader)?

(2)	0
Yes .	No

Total 7

SITUATIONAL CONTROL SCALE

Enter the total scores for the Leader-Member Relations dimension, the Task Structure scale, and the Position Power scale in the spaces below. Add the three scores together and compare your total with the ranges given in the table below to determine your overall situational control.

1. *Leader-Member Relations Total*   16

2. *Task Structure Total*   5

3. *Position Power Total*   7

Grand Total   28

Total Score	51 - 70	31 - 50	10 - 30
Amount of Situational Control	High Control	Moderate Control	Low Control

FEEDBACK ←───────────────

LEADER-MEMBER RELATIONS SCALE

Circle the number which best represents your response to each item.

	strongly agree	agree	neither agree nor disagree	disagree	strongly disagree
1. The people I supervise have trouble getting along with each other.	1	2	③	4	5
2. My subordinates are reliable and trustworthy.	5	4	3	②	1
3. There seems to be a friendly atmosphere among the people I supervise.	5	4	3	②	1
4. My subordinates always cooperate with me in getting the job done.	5	4	③	2	1
5. There is friction between my subordinates and myself.	①	2	3	4	5
6. My subordinates give me a good deal of help and support in getting the job done.	5	4	3	②	1
7. The people I supervise work well together in getting the job done.	5	4	3	2	①
8. I have good relations with the people I supervise.	5	4	3	②	1

Total Score   *

*according to the
interim director's
LMR rating*

FEEDBACK ◄───────────────────────

TASK STRUCTURE RATING SCALE — PART I

Circle the number in the appropriate column.	Usually True	Sometimes True	Seldom True
Is the Goal Clearly Stated or Known?			
1. Is there a blueprint, picture, model or detailed description available of the finished product or service?	2	1	**(0)**
2. Is there a person available to advise and give a description of the finished product or service, or how the job should be done?	2	**(1)**	0
Is There Only One Way to Accomplish the Task?			
3. Is there a step-by-step procedure, or a standard operating procedure which indicates in detail the process which is to be followed?	2	1	**(0)**
4. Is there a specific way to subdivide the task into separate parts or steps?	2	**(1)**	0
5. Are there some ways which are clearly recognized as better than others for performing this task?	2	**(1)**	0
Is There Only One Correct Answer or Solution?			
6. Is is obvious when the task is finished and the correct solution has been found?	2	**(1)**	0
7. Is there a book, manual, or job description which indicates the best solution or the best outcome for the task?	2	1	**(0)**
Is It Easy to Check Whether the Job Was Done Right?			
8. Is there a generally agreed understanding about the standards the particular product or service has to meet to be considered acceptable?	2	**(1)**	0
9. Is the evaluation of this task generally made on some quantitative basis?	2	1	**(0)**
10. Can the leader and the group find out how well the task has been accomplished in enough time to improve future performance?	2	1	**(0)**

SUBTOTAL **5**

FEEDBACK ◄ ─────────────────────────────

TASK STRUCTURE RATING SCALE — PART 2

Training and Experience Adjustment

Note: **Do not adjust jobs with task structure scores of 6 or below.**

(a) Compared to others in this or similar positions, how much *training* has the leader had?

3	2	1	0
No training at all	Very little training	A moderate amount of training	A great deal of training

(b) Compared to others in this or similar positions, how much *experience* has the leader had?

6	4	2	0
No experience at all	Very little experience	A moderate amount of experience	A great deal of experience

Add lines (a) and (b) of the training and experience adjustment, then *subtract* this from the subtotal given in Part 1.

Subtotal from Part 1.

Subtract training and experience adjustment

Total Task Structure Score

FEEDBACK ◄──────────────────────

POSITION POWER RATING SCALE

Circle the number which best represents your answer.

1. Can the leader directly or by recommendation administer rewards and punishments to his subordinates?

2	1	0
Can act directly or can recommend with high effectiveness	Can recommend but with mixed results	No

2. Can the leader directly or by recommendation affect the promotion, demotion, hiring or firing of his subordinates?

2	1	0
Can act directly or can recommend with high effectiveness	Can recommend but with mixed results	No

3. Does the leader have the knowledge necessary to assign tasks to subordinates and instruct them in task completion?

2	1	0
Yes	Sometimes or in some aspects	No

4. Is it the leader's job to evaluate the performance of his subordinates?

2	1	0
Yes	Sometimes or in some aspects	No

5. Has the leader been given some official title of authority by the organization (e.g., foreman, department head, platoon leader)?

2	0
Yes	No

Total $\boxed{7}$

FEEDBACK ◄─────────────────────────

SITUATIONAL CONTROL SCALE

Enter the total scores for the Leader-Member Relations dimension, the Task Structure scale, and the Position Power scale in the spaces below. Add the three scores together and compare your total with the ranges given in the table below to determine your overall situational control.

1. *Leader-Member Relations Total* $\boxed{16}$

2. *Task Structure Total* $\boxed{5}$

3. *Position Power Total* $\boxed{7}$

Grand Total $\boxed{28}$

Total Score	51 - 70	31 - 50	10 - 30
Amount of Situational Control	High Control	Moderate Control	Low Control

FEEDBACK ◄─────────────────────────

If you rated this position as falling into the low control zone (scale value of 28), you were, of course, correct in your assessment. The fact that the research staff was upset and at the point of quitting is compelling information and closely agrees with the *LMR rating of 16*.

The *task structure* is clearly low in this case. A research director's job cannot be considered high in structure, especially when the goal is the development of new products rather than making minor improvement in old products.

The *position power* also should have given you no trouble. A director who can hire and fire has clout. This is, however, mitigated by the fact that the leader in this situation must depend on a staff of experts and that this dependence on their good judgment and willingness to do a good job reduces the power available.

How did you do on these three probes? If you had trouble, review the chapters which gave you the most difficulty. Be sure you understand how to determine situational control before continuing with the program.

If you got all three probes right, you are ready to continue. Review the concepts you have learned in the Part II Summary that follows, and then check your understanding of the program by completing the Part II Self-Test.

SUMMARY OF PART II

In this Part, you were introduced to several new terms used to indicate the amount of control and influence you have over your leadership situation and the outcomes of your decisions. The amount of control you have is determined by evaluating your job on three dimensions:

Leader-Member Relations: How well the group and the leader get along. This is the most important dimension.

Task Structure: The degree to which the job is clearly defined. This is second in importance to leader-member relations and worth half the value in determining situational control.

Position Power: The leader's conferred authority to hire, fire, and discipline which is third in importance in determining situational control.

The combination of these three factors determines situational control, which is divided into three ranges of high, moderate, and low.

High Control: The leader has a great deal of control and influence, exemplified by good leader-member relations, a structured task, and high position power.

Moderate Control: Situations in which the leader typically is presented with mixed problems — either good relations with subordinates but an unstructured task and low position power; or the reverse, poor relations but a structured task and high position power.

Low Control: Situations where the leader's control and influence are relatively low. That is, the group does not support the leader, and neither the task nor position power give the leader much influence. This is more challenging, and for some, a more stressful situation.

You are now ready for Part III, which shows you how to match situations to the leader's personality, as well as a chapter on how to engineer your own leadership situation to fit your leadership style. First, take the Part II Self-Test.

PART II SELF-TEST

1. The second most important factor in determining situational control is

   _____ TASK _____.

2. A situation in which the leader has good relations with his subordinates and an unstructured task with low position power would be one of

   high/moderate/low _____ situational control.

3. The scale used to measure your relations with your group is called

   Leader member relations

4. A situation in which the leader has poor leader-member relations, low position power, and an unstructured task would be one of

   high/moderate/low _____ situational control.

5. The amount of authority you have in a given situation can be measured

   by the _Position power_ scale.

6. The three dimensions used to determine situational control in order of their importance are as follows (check the correct choice):

   ___ (a) 1. Task Structure   ___ (b) 1. Leader-Member Relations
       2. Position Power   2. Position Power
       3. Leader-Member Relations   3. Task Structure

              ___ (c) 1. Leader-Member Relations
                      2. Task Structure
                      3. Position Power

7. A situation in which the leader has good leader-member relations, high position power, and a structured task would be one of

   high/moderate/low _____ situational control.

Answers to Part II Self-Test

The correct answers to the Part II Self-Test are:

1. task structure

2. moderate situational control

3. LMR scale

4. low situational control

5. position power scale

6. (c)

7. high situational control

If you missed any of these items, be sure to review the relevant material before you go on.

PART III
Creating the Optimal Leadership Environment

CHAPTER EIGHT

Matching Your Leadership Style with Your Situation

The previous chapters gave you specific instructions on determining the degree of control of various leadership situations. Effective leadership requires that you match the situation to your particular leadership style. In this chapter we will discuss the type of leadership situation which goes best with each type of leadership style. You will also determine the situational control for your primary job. The next chapters will deal with ways in which you can modify your leadership situation to fit your leadership style and ways in which you can apply your training to the management of leaders who work under your direction.

As mentioned earlier, very few leaders are fortunate enough to function equally well in all situations and under all conditions. Now that you know your own leadership style, you are ready to identify the kinds of situations in which you perform best.

The appropriate match between leadership style and situational control is shown below:

1. Task-motivated (low LPC) leaders perform best in situations of high control or low control.

2. Relationship-motivated (high LPC) leaders perform best in situations of moderate control.

Before we go on, let us just briefly review once more the three categories of situational control:

1. *High Control:* These are the situations in which leaders have a predictable environment, that is, situations in which he or she has the support of the group members as well as a task which is highly structured so that everyone knows exactly what to do and how to do it. In addition, leaders have relatively high position power which enables them to back up their authority with appropriate rewards and punishment. In other words, leaders have a great deal of control and influence and can feel reasonably secure and certain that (a) their directions will be followed, and (b) their decisions will have the intended outcomes. *This situation is best for the low LPC leader.*

2. *Moderate Control:*   These situations generally present mixed problems. Leaders may be supported by their group, but the task is relatively ambiguous and unstructured, and formal authority weak. Alternatively the task might be structured and clear-cut, and the position power high, but the group members are nonsupportive. The leader, therefore, has to be diplomatic and tactful and concerned with the feelings of the group members in order to get their cooperation. *This situation is best for the high LPC leader.*

3. *Low Control:*   These situations are relatively difficult, more challenging, and sometimes quite stressful. The task is likely to be unstructured and unclear, and there are likely to be no definite procedures or methods. Most importantly, leaders will feel that their group members do not like or support them and that they have little or no formal power to help them get things done. Even when they do have formal power and a structured task, a situation in which stress and anxiety are very high gives them little control and assurance that they can determine the outcome. Some people prefer this kind of situation because they enjoy the challenge. *This situation is best for the low LPC leader.*

The table on the next page summarizes the match between situations and different leadership styles.

If your leadership style and the situational control are properly matched, your performance as well as the group's output should be good. However, if you are mismatched with your situational control, you may not be performing very well, and you may also become quite dissatisfied or discouraged with your job. If you are mismatched, the next chapter will help you determine how to change your situation. If you are in the right situation for your leadership style, the next chapter will tell you how to keep it that way.

Be sure to remember that the various scales for scoring and classifying situational control are guidelines, not ironclad rules. You must use your own judgment because there may well be some situations in which leader-member relations are so poor that the situation is low in control even though task structure and position power are high. There may also be situations in which position power is so strong that the other factors matter very little (a general supervising a team of enlisted men), or task structure is so high that leader-member relations and position power count for very little (e.g., the person in charge of a countdown of a space probe).

By this time you should have enough experience estimating the three dimensions that you can apply the theory without using the specific scales. In the remainder of the program, you will not be filling out scales to complete the probes; rather you will be basing your decisions on your understanding of the *Leader Match* program. If you have difficulty with a particular probe or would feel more confident in applying the theory, use the extra scales reproduced from the master copies provided in the appendix. However,

Summary of Leadership Style, Behavior, and Performance in Varying Situations

Leader Type	SITUATIONAL CONTROL		
	High Control	Moderate Control	Low Control
High LPC	*Behavior:* Somewhat autocratic, aloof and self-centered. Seemingly concerned with task. *Performance:* Poor	*Behavior:* Considerate, open, and participative. *Performance:* Good	*Behavior:* Anxious, tentative, overly concerned with interpersonal relations. *Performance:* Poor
Low LPC	*Behavior:* Considerate, and supportive. *Performance:* Good.	*Behavior:* Tense, task-focused. *Performance:* Poor.	*Behavior:* Directive, task-focused, serious. *Performance:* Relatively good.

you should be able to diagnose situational control quickly and accurately so that you don't have to spend a lot of time with complex scales. The following probes illustrate the matching concept.

Some leadership styles do not match the situation.

—————————————————————————————→ **PROBE 18**

You are the personnel director of a large company. A job has opened up for a middle-level manager in the accounting department which involves the supervision of several sections. All sections perform relatively routine book-keeping, billing, and record keeping tasks. You consider this task highly structured and this evaluation is confirmed by several managers who completed the task structure scale. You have every reason to believe that morale and employee satisfaction are high and that the department has generally had good relations between supervisors and employees. Moreover, the supervisors who would be reporting to the new manager are cooperative and eager to get along with management. Since the manager will have considerable authority, the position power is clearly high. Thus, situational control of the leadership position should be quite high. Most managers in the position stayed there for five or six years.

You have the job files on a number of junior executives who are eligible for this job and you are asked to make a recommendation.

Randolph Wallingford has been with the company for about five years. During the early years of his managerial career he held several staff jobs which were unstructured and which he performed passably well. He was then assigned to a management position of an accounting section in a branch office where he stayed for about one year. His performance again was passable but not distinguished.

He was then reassigned to manage an accounts receivable section, a structured and fairly routine job, where he has been for almost three years. He had a slow start but has become quite effective in the last year.

His subordinates feel that he is hard to get to know, although they like to work for him, and as long as they do their job he is easy to get along with. The LPC scale he completed on joining the firm indicates that he is task-motivated.

Joan Redmond is something of a company success story. Her first job was as assistant manager of the data processing department where she suggested a number of new procedures which have been adopted. She requested a transfer after one year to a new billing department and again performed quite well. She seemed to run down after about two years and requested a transfer to sales. She seems to be seeking new and interesting jobs which she feels broaden her experience.

Her fellow workers consider Joan easy to get along with, approachable, pleasant, and eager to make a good impression. Routine jobs tend to turn her off. Her LPC scale verifies that she is relationship-motivated.

John Leshi has held only one job in the company. When he first took the job, which involved keeping track of shipping and purchasing schedules, his performance was somewhat below the company's expectations, although his relations with co-workers were fairly good and he never had any major problems. He has remained in the same job without much improvement, and has not asked for a transfer or a promotion. His job calls for no particular ingenuity, and he has shown no interest to make more of it. His leadership style is relationship-motivated according to his LPC score.

Considering that this is a high control situation, you decide to select:

_____ ✓ (a) Wallingford.

_____ (b) Redmond.

_____ (c) Leshi.

Go to the next page for feedback.

FEEDBACK ◄─────────────────────

a **You chose (a):** *Randolph Wallingford.* This is a good selection. His history of low performance in new and unstructured situations, or when first assigned to a management position confirms that he is task-motivated. This is further supported by the report that he is detached, hard to get to know, although easy to get along with as long as everyone does their job.

The leadership situation in the accounting department obviously provides high position power and high task structure. This is an ideal position for a task-motivated manager. Since most managers have stayed in this position for five or six years it would certainly be worthwhile to prefer Wallingford, who is likely to become increasingly better as time goes on.

Notice here that LPC scales were available in company files and that you were able to verify the leadership style from the descriptions of his behavior. As we've said before, you should try whenever possible to obtain LPC scores because that is the most accurate way to determine leadership style. .

Good work! Now try Probe 19 on the next page.

b **You chose (b):** *Joan Redmond.* This is probably not the best choice. You can check that Redmond is relationship-motivated because, in the new situations which she seeks out, she is easy to work with, approachable, pleasant, and eager to make a good impression. However, relationship-motivated people do not perform well in high control situations, and her history of asking for frequent transfers would indicate that she would not want to remain in the job as long as 5 or 6 years.

Go back to page 139 and make another choice.

c **You chose (c):** *John Leshi.* This is not such a good choice. From all indications, Leshi has held a structured job with high position power for several years and failed to improve. He seems a pleasant enough person but this is not one of the prime requisites of the job. His motivation seems questionable, so there is no reason to expect that Leshi will somehow blossom forth in a more difficult and demanding job which this promotion would entail.

Go back to page 139 and make another choice.

→ **PROBE 19**

You are the Director of a large manufacturing firm. The manager in charge of the advertising department just had a serious accident and has to be replaced since it is doubtful that he will be able to return to work for quite some time. You need someone who will fill in for him.

The situation is rather hard to define. The key people are temperamental and touchy, and there has been a great deal of infighting and conflict. The manager has had a difficult time holding the department together. Moreover, there has been a demand from other managers for more creative marketing campaigns. You need someone who can immediately take charge of this department and make it productive.

What kind of leader will you choose?

_____ (a) You pick a task-motivated (low LPC) leader.

_____ (b) You try to find a relationship-motivated (high LPC) person.

FEEDBACK ←────────────────────────

(a) **You chose (a):** *You pick a task-motivated (low LPC) leader.* This is the correct choice. Low LPC persons tend to perform best in situations in which their control and influence are low. You noted that there is a great deal of tension and conflict among the key people in the department, which suggests that the support which these employees will give to their manager will be unreliable at best, and probably quite poor. The task structure of an advertising department is very low, especially since there is a demand for more creative marketing, which places additional stress on this unstructured task. Finally, the fact that the manager has been trying to hold the department together, implies that he has been in danger of losing some of his important subordinates. The group's loyalty is, therefore, likely to be low. While the manager might have some formal position power, it would be very difficult to rely on disciplinary measures to keep the group in line. This is, therefore, clearly a low control situation.

You're doing well; now try Probe 20 on the next page.

(b) **You chose (b):** *You try to find a relationship-motivated (high LPC) person.* This is not the best answer. The manager of the advertising department has a very unstructured task, and he or she is under considerable pressure to come up with some creative new solutions to marketing problems. Under ordinary conditions, given good relations with subordinates and the typical power of a manager, this would call for a relationship-motivated leader. In this case, however, the situation provides the manager with very poor control. Not only is the task unstructured, but the key people in the group are engaged in infighting and are not likely to give their wholehearted support to their manager. No matter which side the manager takes, somebody in the group will attack him for it. Moreover, the statement that the manager has been trying to keep his department together suggests that the manager is in a very weak position since he must placate and appease his subordinates. Even if the department manager had formal power to reward and punish, he probably could not really use it under these conditions. A relationship-motivated leader would not be able to work too well in this situation.

Now try Probe 20.

 **PROBE 20**

You are a Vice-President of an electronics firm with plants in eight cities across the country. Recently several incidents have occurred which appear to indicate a breach of security procedures in the patent products division on the West Coast. You must select a member of your staff and two others to go to the west coast plant to investigate the problem.

Here are some of the factors which should be considered:

1. The local plant director and security officials are expected to be unhappy to have an outside investigation. One aspect of the case is the possibility that the problem occurred because they paid inadequate attention to their duties.

2. This is a large facility with a heavy production schedule, so the investigation will have to be quite broad. Some standard investigative procedures will, of course, be followed but many decisions will have to be made as the investigation proceeds.

3. The head of the investigative team you send out will be given a special title and will have the major responsibility to recommend any procedural and personnel changes.

To decide which member of your staff is to head the team, you must first consider the situational control of the investigation. Based on your best, off-the-cuff judgment, what is the situational control of this assignment?

___✓___ Low Control

___✓___ Moderate Control

_____ High Control

Given this situation, which of the following staff members would you choose as having the best chance of successfully accomplishing this assignment?

___ Margaret Anderson - High LPC (Relationship-motivated).

___✓ Randy Brannigan - Low LPC (Task-motivated).

Feedback is given on the following page.

FEEDBACK ◄──────────────────────────

The situation suggests, first of all, that the task structure will be relatively low. The team will have to make decisions as the investigation progresses. Since the head of the team will be quite dependent upon his or her fellow team members, the position power also is likely to be low. However, a team of three people, forced to work in a relatively hostile environment (who likes an investigation?) is likely to stick together, and the leader-member relations are, therefore, apt to be quite good. This suggests that the assignment would have moderate situational control. Margaret Anderson would, therefore, be your best choice, especially since high LPC people are able to manage somewhat better in difficult interpersonal situations, and investigating a problem of this nature is likely to be just that.

COMPUTING SITUATIONAL CONTROL FOR YOUR PRIMARY LEADERSHIP JOB

Now that you have had considerable practice with all of the scales which measure the various aspects of leadership control and have determined your leadership style, you are ready to analyze your *primary* leadership situation.

On the following pages are scales which you should complete to determine the amount of control you have in your primary leadership situation — either your present leadership job or your most important past leadership role. Score each scale, and then compute the overall rating. Locate your score on the table to determine the amount of situational control for this job.

The next chapter will discuss what to do if you find that your primary leadership job does not match your leadership style or, if you are in the right situation, how to maintain this successful match.

LEADER-MEMBER RELATIONS SCALE

Circle the number which best represents your response to each item.

	strongly agree	agree	neither agree nor disagree	disagree	strongly disagree
1. The people I supervise have trouble getting along with each other.	1	2	3	(4)	5
2. My subordinates are reliable and trustworthy.	5	(4)	3	2	1
3. There seems to be a friendly atmosphere among the people I supervise.	5	(4)	3	2	1
4. My subordinates always cooperate with me in getting the job done.	5	4	(3)	2	1
5. There is friction between my subordinates and myself.	1	2	(3)	4	5
6. My subordinates give me a good deal of help and support in getting the job done.	5	4	(3)	2	1
7. The people I supervise work well together in getting the job done.	5	(4)	3	2	1
8. I have good relations with the people I supervise.	5	4	(3)	2	1

16
12

Total Score 28

TASK STRUCTURE RATING SCALE — PART I

Circle the number in the appropriate column.

	Usually True	Sometimes True	Seldom True
Is the Goal Clearly Stated or Known?			
1. Is there a blueprint, picture, model or detailed description available of the finished product or service?	2	1	(0)
2. Is there a person available to advise and give a description of the finished product or service, or how the job should be done?	(2)	1	0
Is There Only One Way to Accomplish the Task?			
3. Is there a step-by-step procedure, or a standard operating procedure which indicates in detail the process which is to be followed?	2	(1)	0
4. Is there a specific way to subdivide the task into separate parts or steps?	2	(1)	0
5. Are there some ways which are clearly recognized as better than others for performing this task?	(2)	1	0
Is There Only One Correct Answer or Solution?			
6. Is it obvious when the task is finished and the correct solution has been found?	(2)	1	0
7. Is there a book, manual, or job description which indicates the best solution or the best outcome for the task?	2	1	(0)
Is It Easy to Check Whether the Job Was Done Right?			
8. Is there a generally agreed understanding about the standards the particular product or service has to meet to be considered acceptable?	(2)	1	0
9. Is the evaluation of this task generally made on some quantitative basis?	2	1	(0)
10. Can the leader and the group find out how well the task has been accomplished in enough time to improve future performance?	(2)	1	0

SUBTOTAL   12

TASK STRUCTURE RATING SCALE — PART 2

Training and Experience Adjustment

NOTE: Do not adjust jobs with task structure scores of 6 or below.

(a)   Compared to others in this or similar positions, how much *training* has the leader had?

3	(2)	1	0
No training at all	Very little training	A moderate amount of training	A great deal of training

(b)   Compared to others in this or similar positions, how much *experience* has the leader had?

6	4	(2)	0
No experience at all	Very little experience	A moderate amount of experience	A great deal of experience

Add lines (a) and (b) of the training and experience adjustment, then *subtract* this from the subtotal given in Part 1.

Subtotal from Part 1. | 12 |

Subtract training and experience adjustment | −4 |

Total Task Structure Score | 8 |

POSITION POWER RATING SCALE

Circle the number which best represents your answer.

1. Can the leader directly or by recommendation administer rewards and punishments to his subordinates?

2	1	0
Can act directly or can recommend with high effectiveness	Can recommend but with mixed results	No

2. Can the leader directly or by recommendation affect the promotion, demotion, hiring or firing of his subordinates?

2	1	0
Can act directly or can recommend with high effectiveness	Can recommend but with mixed results	No

3. Does the leader have the knowledge necessary to assign tasks to subordinates and instruct them in task completion?

2	1	0
Yes	Sometimes or in some aspects	No

4. Is it the leader's job to evaluate the performance of his subordinates?

2	1	0
Yes	Sometimes or in some aspects	No

5. Has the leader been given some official title of authority by the organization (e.g., foreman, department head, platoon leader)?

2	0
Yes	No

Total   8

SITUATIONAL CONTROL SCALE

Enter the total scores for the Leader-Member Relations dimension, the Task Structure scale, and the Position Power scale in the spaces below. Add the three scores together and compare your total with the ranges given in the table below to determine your overall situational control.

1. *Leader-Member Relations Total*   28

2. *Task Structure Total*   8

3. *Position Power Total*   8

Grand Total   44

Total Score	51 - 70	31 - 50	10 - 30
Amount of Situational Control	High Control	Moderate Control	Low Control

SUMMARY

The basic problem in leadership performance is the appropriate match between the leader's style or motivational pattern and the degree to which the leadership situation provides the leader with control and influence. As we said before, task-motivated leaders tend to perform best in high control and low control situations, and relationship-motivated leaders perform best in moderate control situations.

The problem for leaders consists of getting into, and remaining in, situations in which they can perform well. Knowing your leadership style and being able to identify the amount of control of the situation enables you to do this. Equally important, it should also make you aware of situations in which you are less likely to perform well. Remember, if you learn to avoid situations in which you are likely to fail, you're bound to be a success. The next chapter will discuss what to do if your leadership style and situational control do not make an appropriate match.

Learn to avoid situations in which you are likely to fail.

Engineering Your Own Leadership Situation

You will sometimes find yourself in situations which do not match your particular leadership style. When this occurs you have two choices: You can change your leadership style — and your personality which determines your style — or you can modify your leadership situation.

Let us remember, first of all, that your basic leadership style is part of your personality. It is the ingrained pattern of behavior which you adopt when dealing with others above or below you in authority. This is as much a part of your personality as the way you behave toward your parents, or your children. How easy is it to change your basic leadership style? Practically speaking, it would be as difficult as suddenly trying to become a completely different person. Your personality, and therefore your leadership style, have been developing all your life, and it is as difficult to change one as the other.

It is much easier to change your situation. Your ability to do this is considerably greater than you may realize, and job engineering provides an important method for improving your own leadership performance and the effectiveness of your organization. How this can be done is the main topic of this chapter.

How much you can modify or "engineer" your own leadership job depends on a number of factors. If your relationship with your boss allows you to talk freely with him, and if he is supportive, you may be more successful in changing a number of important dimensions of your leadership job. And remember, your good performance reflects well on him!

If your relationship is strained, your ability to make changes in your leadership situation will be more limited. If possible, you should sit down with your boss and discuss with him the kinds of situations which seem to be most suitable for you, and discuss with him the various ways in which you both could restructure your leadership situation so that it matches your particular leadership style. If your relationship with your boss does not permit you to do this, you will have to try to make some of the changes on your own.

Not surprisingly, the three components of the job situation — leader-member relations, task structure, and position power — are the areas in which you can modify your leadership situation. The three areas are dealt with below along with checklists of options which you may use to engineer your job situation.

MODIFYING LEADER-MEMBER RELATIONS

Some people naturally and easily establish a climate of goodwill and trust with their subordinates and develop close and lasting friendships with them. For others this is more difficult. If you wish to improve your leader-member relations, make sure that you clearly understand your subordinates' problems and that you try to alleviate them. You can become socially more accessible to them so that they get to know you as a person, and you can try to provide them with accurate information about the organization so that you earn their trust and confidence. You might institute special "gripe sessions" or regular meetings to give your subordinates an opportunity to know you better. You might institute informal brown-bag lunches or occasionally go out after work with them to celebrate the successful completion of a particular task.

If you are fortunate enough to establish good leader-member relations easily, you may be reluctant to jeopardize these relations in order to have a more effective group. However, leader-member relations can become too close for effective task performance. Group members may complain about favoritism, or you may find that you cannot properly discipline a subordinate because he or she is your friend. It may then be necessary to increase the distance between your group and yourself.

For example, one Air Force commander noted that the aircraft maintenance of his unit had become sloppy. He had been having lunch with his

You can get closer to your subordinates by socializing with them.

maintenance officers and had developed a very friendly relationship with them. He began to suspect that the maintenance officers were banking on their friendship with him to get them by. The commander realized that his own career would be on the line if he permitted poor work to continue.

As his way of handling this problem he *gradually* stopped socializing with his maintenance officers. This created some concern ("Why is George no longer coming around?" "Does he still think I am doing a good job?"). These anxieties soon became translated into more careful work and greater efforts to perform good maintenance, with the result that the maintenance service markedly improved within a relatively short time. When a boss withdraws from social contact, he makes it difficult for the subordinate to assure himself of his boss' approval in any way except by good performance.

Another officer knew he was extremely good at handling the "difficult cases," the less-motivated employees. He told his commander that he would be willing to take some of the most troublesome enlisted men in his unit, to the delight of all concerned. This made his situation more challenging and lowered his control over the situation. *His performance increased* and the officer was given an early promotion.

As we said earlier in Chapter Three, your relations with your group members are the most important dimension of situational control and they are, therefore, given the most weight. Changes you make in this dimension will have a greater effect on situational control than will changes in either task structure or position power.

Leaders are often unaware of the possible changes they can make in their leadership situation. They assume that such changes are impossible. A check list for leader-member relations follows. You should carefully go over this list and *make a checkmark* beside each action which may be available to you.

Checklist for Changing Your Leader-Member Relations

_____✓_____ Spend more — or less — informal time with your subordinates (e.g., lunch, leisure activities, etc.).

_____ Organize some off-work group activities which include your subordinates (e.g., picnics, bowling, softball teams, excursions, etc.).

_____✓_____ Request particular people for work in your group.

_____ Volunteer to direct difficult or troublesome subordinates.

_____ Suggest or effect transfers of particular subordinates into or out of your unit.

_____✓_____ Raise morale by obtaining positive outcomes for subordinates (e.g., special bonuses, time off, attractive jobs).

_____✓_____ Increase or decrease your availability to subordinates (e.g., open door policy, special gripe sessions, time available for personal consultation).

_____ Share information "from above" freely with your subordinates.

Leaders have essentially two options open to them which might affect leader-member relations. The first of these is to change the actual membership of the group. This option is very effective but is rarely available to most leaders. The second option is to increase or decrease the rapport between the leader and subordinates by affecting the time spent together, the leader's concern and interest, and the leader's actions to increase the morale and well-being of the unit. These latter actions are generally open to any leader who feels comfortable and effective in using them.

MODIFYING TASK STRUCTURE

This dimension, too, permits you to modify your leadership situation to a certain degree. While the job assigned to your group may well be out of your control, you usually have some choice in how to approach it.

If you wish to work with a more highly structured task you can:

1. ask your superior to give you, whenever possible, the tasks which are more structured or to give you more detailed instructions;

2. learn all you can about the task so that you can prepare a detailed plan for performing the job, and get additional instruction and expert guidance if needed;

3. break the job down into smaller subtasks which can be more highly structured;

4. volunteer for structured tasks, and avoid the unstructured ones;

5. obtain further training;

6. develop procedures, guidelines, diagrams, or outlines complete with examples of previous jobs where possible.

A glance at the task structure rating scale shows that any action which increases the clarity of the job will increase structure. If you wish to work with a less structured task, you can:

1. ask your boss, whenever possible, to give you the new or unusual problems and let you figure out how to get them done;

2. bring the problems and tasks to your group members and invite them to work with you on the planning and decision-making phases of the task;

3. where possible, leave the task in relatively vague form. The ideal method of dealing with this part of the task is, of course, to work through your boss;

4. volunteer for unstructured tasks and try to avoid structured work assignments.

Task structure is the second most important dimension of situational control. Be aware that changes you make in this dimension may not always be sufficient to increase or decrease situational control to the desired level. In many cases, it may be necessary to change both task structure and position power to achieve the desired effect.

Checklist for Changing Your Task Structure

Go over this list and check the options which are available to you.

1. Training

_____ Volunteer or request assignment to formal organizational training programs.

_____ Enroll in training programs outside the organization through local schools, universities, adult education, or correspondence courses.

___✓___ Study books or training manuals prepared by the organization.

_____ Research books available outside the organization, such as in local libraries.

___✓___ Try to obtain informal training from co-workers or superiors (Is there an experienced person around who would be willing to give you some tips or background?).

_____ Approach the job in an open, unstructured way without any preconceptions.

2. Developing procedures, criteria, and feedback. The task structure rating scale makes it clear that any action which can increase the clarity and specificity of procedures, criteria, and feedback will increase task structure. Listed below are some ways of accomplishing those actions.

___✓___ Request clearer guidelines from your superior.

_____ Use available expert personnel within the organization (e.g., expert subordinates, peers, experienced co-workers).

___✓___ Keep records of all aspects of the job. Attempt to increase structure by observation and systematization of regular or repeated trends.

___✓___ Develop subgoals, individually or with the help of superiors, peers, and subordinates, which provide short-range criteria and feedback.

_____ Lower structure by involving a number of people with differing viewpoints to work and comment on the project. This will increase the complexity of the problem by providing a greater number of possible ways to proceed.

3. Experience

_____ Request transfer. Frequent transfers keeps the job fresh and new and does not allow extensive experience to accumulate.

_____ Refuse or avoid transfers.

_____ Volunteer for long-range assignments.

___✓___ Make the most of experience by keeping accurate records of job-related activities.

MODIFYING POSITION POWER

While position power is defined as the power and authority which the organization vests in your leadership position, there are some ways you can change your position power, though not all of these will work in every case.

To raise your position power, you can:

1. show your subordinates "who's boss" by exercising fully the powers which the organization provides;

2. become, as quickly as possible, an expert on the job (e.g., through training) so that you can appropriately evaluate subordinates' performance, and not have to depend on others in the group to assist you in planning and organizing the job;

3. make sure that information to your group gets channeled through you.

To lower your position power, you can:

1. try to be "one of the gang" by socializing, by playing down any trappings of power and rank the organization may have given you;

2. call on members of your group to participate in planning and decision-making functions. (This is essentially what participative management is about; it requires the leader to share decision-making);

3. let information from the organization reach all group members as quickly and directly as possible and permit group members easy access to your boss (sometimes an uncomfortable path!);

4. let your assistants exercise relatively more power.

Position power has comparatively less weight than the other two dimensions of situational control. Changes in position power alone will often be insufficient to make a difference. You may also have to change task structure or leader-member relations to achieve the desired change in situational control.

Checklist for Changing Your Position Power

Make a check mark by those actions which may be appropriate to your situation. Position power derives primarily from organizational procedures and policies and cannot generally be drastically changed. However, subtle but effective changes can often be made.

_____ ✓ Be flexible in giving rewards and punishment.

_____ ✓ Delegate authority to subordinates and allow them to share in decision-making.

_____ ✓ Request aid or assistance from superiors to augment your authority.

_____ ✓ Utilize assistants to delegate some of your disciplinary responsibilities.

In trying to engineer your job you must, of course, be aware that certain changes you make are very difficult to undo. You cannot play the part of the "heavy" one day and the sociable, approachable boss the next day. Moreover, changes of this type should be made tentatively and in small steps so that you can gauge how far you should go for maximum effect. This is a job for a scalpel and not a meat axe.

It is generally unwise to make a situation deliberately low in control. Regardless of their leadership style, leaders and their groups often perform less well in situations of very low leader control or high stress than in moderate control or high control situations.

The most important point, however, is to re-evaluate your situation periodically after you have made adjustments to see if further fine-tuning is needed. You may find, for example, that you've made the situation too high in control, and further adjustment may be necessary. Or you may not have increased your situational control enough to improve performance, and you may need to make additional changes.

Continuous monitoring is essential to maintain high group effectiveness. And above all, remember: Don't change your situation if you are performing effectively — _If it runs well, don't fix it!_

→ **PROBE 21**

You are a captain commanding an armored company. You are aware that your commanding officer has not been too happy with your performance in the last few months.

In analyzing your job you note that you have considerable power in assigning and disciplining people, you can recommend promotions and your superior usually follows your recommendations. You seem to get along well with everyone and in fact, you know that you are well liked. You also know your job well. All things considered, this is a very high control situation.

You find that you are particularly good at resolving conflict, and when the unit was new you used to be very concerned with the welfare of your group, but over the last few months you have become aloof from them. However, in the past when things have gone poorly, you talked about your problems, and sought out the people in your work group for reassurance.

1. Your leadership style is most likely to be:

   ✓ relationship-motivated

   _____ task-motivated

2. As a way of increasing your performance, you could do one or more of the following:

   _____ (a) Ask your commanding officer for a more difficult task to increase your job stress.

   ✓ (b) Ask for some of the troublemakers in the organization to be transferred to your work group.

   _____ (c) Seek advice and assistance from individuals who have had prior command in an armored company.

Feedback is given on the following page.

FEEDBACK ◄─────────────────────────

1. Your leadership style is probably *relationship-motivated*. This is indicated by your past ability to resolve conflicts and work closely with your subordinates. Your present problems with subordinates are probably the effects of extended job experience. Your experience has helped to structure the job, moving you into a very high control leadership situation. In such high control situations, relationship-motivated (high LPC) leaders are likely to become disinterested or self-centered and lose rapport with their subordinates. (If you had trouble with this question, review the discussion of leader types on pages 8-9.)

2. Having determined that you are relationship-motivated and you now are in a very high control situation, you would somehow want to move into a zone of moderate control which matches your leadership style.

   One means for achieving that effect might be to ask your commanding officer to assign you the difficult men in his command. You might also ask him to give you a more challenging task to increase your job stress. You could also put yourself under greater pressure by setting tight deadlines, or developing new training methods.

   Getting advice on how to do your job would make the situation even more highly controlled and this might make your performance problem even worse.

   Because job engineering is the key to the effectiveness of this training program, if you had trouble with this probe, reread Chapter Nine before continuing. If you got this one right, you are doing well; try Probe 22 on the next page.

————————————————————————→ **PROBE 22**

You are a foreman who supervises assembly line workers. You have an LPC score of 78; you are relationship-motivated. You were promoted up from the assembly line two years ago and your group's performance was very good at the outset. You received the regular company training programs and seem to know the job quite well. In the last six months the group's output has fallen slightly and there appears to be a slow decline in performance. You have completed a situational control rating and determined your situation as "very high control."

Which courses of action might be most advantageous for you?

_____ (a)   Stop worrying. The downward trend in performance will probably reverse itself.

_____ (b)   Ask your boss to assign you some of the more difficult people in the plant.

_____ (c)   Talk to your boss about increasing your position power by allowing you to hire your own people.

_____ (d)   Seek additional training.

_____ (e)   Ask for a transfer to a new job with greater responsibility.

_____ (f)   Ask for a transfer to another structured job with new subordinates, e.g., a different shift.

FEEDBACK ←———————————————————————

Your preferred courses of action would probably be choices (b), (e), or (f). All of these choices would have the effect of lowering situational control to more appropriately match the foreman's style. The other choices improve situational control — which is exactly opposite to the best course of action.

Of the three potentially valid choices, either (e) or (f) is preferable to (b). A transfer to a new situation is probably the best way to improve performance for a relationship-motivated leader. The foreman has indicated that he is quick to learn and gain control of his situation. Promotion, if possible, would place him in a new and challenging situation and does not involve any negative actions.

If you are still having problems with job engineering, be sure to review Chapter Nine before continuing. If you got this probe right, keep up the good work and continue!

DOES SITUATIONAL CONTROL CHANGE?

We have spoken of the control of your job situation as if it were merely the result of the situation, that is, that the situation provides you with control and influence to the extent to which (a) you have good relationships with your subordinates, (b) your task is structured, and (c) you have position power to direct the work of others.

A moment's reflection will tell you, however, that your situational control is likely to change over time. First of all, you typically do not step into a leadership job in which the group immediately gives you ardent support. Support usually has to be earned, and this requires time. Second, and perhaps more importantly, even the most structured task has to be learned, either by experience or by training.

This point will be readily apparent to those who have done much work in the kitchen. Just pick up a cookbook, and turn to souffles or a similar recipe. The directions are all described in step-by-step detail: " . . . separate yolks and whites of six eggs . . . beat egg yolks with sugar and lemon juice until light and fluffy . . . blend in sifted flour . . . beat egg whites until stiff . . . and fold-in egg yolk . . . "

Now, how do you separate yolks and whites? And what is "light and fluffy," and how do you "fold-in" egg yolk? After you've cooked for a while you will know what these terms mean and you will learn how to perform the various operations without too much trouble. Your initial bewilderment will gradually give way to a feeling of competence. In effect, the task will have become more structured for you, and you will be less flustered and anxious as you go about following the various instructions.

A similar process occurs, of course, with nearly every new job you undertake. It takes a while to learn the ropes, and no matter how exact the instructions might be, innumerable problems require you to improvise and innovate, or to find out from others how your predecessors managed.

Clearly, then, you have less control when you begin a new job than after you have been at work for some time. As a rule of thumb, assume that a job which is high in control for the *experienced* leader will be only moderate in situational control for the inexperienced, new leader. Assume that the job which is moderate for the leader who has been on the job for some time, will be low in control for the new leader.

This can be illustrated as follows:

Experienced Leader:	High Control	Moderate Control	Low Control
New Leader:	Moderate Control	Low Control	Extremely Low Control

Your leadership situation is a dynamic, constantly changing affair which needs careful monitoring. While you may be appropriately matched with your leadership style right now, your situation may change within a month or a year, and you may find that you are not performing as well as before, or that the job is boring you and is less challenging.

Job engineering is not something you can do once, and then forget. It requires constant attention and constant adjustments. Even if the specifications, themselves, do not change, your ability to deal with the job is likely to change. Generally speaking, the job is likely to become more routine over time; it will become "easier" to do, but also less challenging, thus requiring less of your attention. Your problem is to maintain a continuous balance in which your leadership style keeps matching your leadership situation.

CONSIDERING A NEW LEADERSHIP POSITION

When you are first approached with an offer to take a new leadership job, frequently as a promotion to a higher or more desirable position, your options are usually limited. You frequently will know less about the job than you would like to know. For example, who will be your subordinates; what kind of a person is your new boss; how much authority will you have?

Even if you are asked to move to a job you know well, declining it may mean that you may have a long time to wait before another promotion might come your way. On the other hand, you may have more leeway in making the situation fit you than first meets the eye. Let us examine the various options which might be available to you.

At best, you may be able to learn enough about the job to know that the situational control is likely to match your leadership style. In this case, of course, you should accept the new job with enthusiasm but be aware that you may become less effective as your increasing experience and knowledge on the job change the degree of control you can exercise.

You may decide that the situational control of the prospective job is a mismatch for your leadership style. Rather than risking failure, you may decline the move and explain to your boss that this is not likely to be a job in which you can do your best. This is a tough choice to make, and it usually should not be made only on the basis that the leadership situation does not match your leadership style. It does happen, however, that there are people who simply do not want to become bogged down with more administrative and managerial responsibilities. Many research scientists in charge of small teams do not want to give up their work in order to become directors of large laboratories, and many teachers don't want to become principals. In many of these cases the individual who is tapped for the job simply does not feel that he could be as satisfied or effective in a higher managerial position.

You may decide that you are probably mismatched for the situation for which you are slated, but that you can make a number of changes so that the job will suit you. This is a frequent situation in which the candidate for the job says in effect, "I'll take it if you will let me . . . " This will usually require a discussion with your boss or with your future boss in which you explore whether you could modify certain aspects of the job (e.g., bring one of your people along as an executive assistant, report directly to Mr. X, have authority to move your immediate staff members).

It may also be possible that your job will allow you to make all the required changes informally without consulting your new boss. For example, you may arrange the work so that you create considerable distance between yourself and your subordinates by being rather formal with them, by having them go through your assistant, or by seeing them only on appointment. On the other hand, you may make yourself easily available, see them informally and socially, and become one of the group.

You may actively seek maximum support from your boss (for example, direct access), either as a condition of taking the job, or by keeping in close communication with him or her. Alternatively, you may decide not to lean on your boss for support, and to rely, instead, on yourself or the members of your group. In this case you may want the boss to define your sphere of authority. You could also bring one or more assistants with you who will give you the support you may need from immediate subordinates; or, alternatively, bring in people who can play the devil's advocate.

You may, over time, change the types of jobs which are offered to you. This is possible in some organizations, and quite out of the question in others. However, you will almost certainly have some options in how you organize the group's task and how the task will, therefore, be structured.

Finally, you may modify your leadership situation by training, by experience, and by obtaining expert help from others in the organization. Thus, if you are a low LPC leader who has been moved into a situation of moderate control, you may increase the control by seeking relevant job training, coaching, or by breaking the tasks down into smaller, more manageable components. If you are a high LPC leader operating in a situation of relatively high control, you might consider a participative management approach in which you share planning and decision-making functions with others in your group; you might look for more challenging jobs or assignments for your department. You might also restructure your group by including inexperienced members who will need to be trained.

All the strategies which we have mentioned present certain problems. (We never said that leadership was simple!) If you only take on those jobs which best fit you, you may deprive yourself of a chance to grow in your leadership experience and to learn how to cope with new problems. You may also feel that a leader who doesn't take on every job, whether or not he feels particularly suited for it, is shirking his responsibility.

These are complex issues. You certainly might want to try some leadership jobs that may not be exactly suited to you just to see how you measure up to the difficulties. There is nothing wrong with this approach as long as you know what you are doing. You will certainly benefit if you monitor your performance carefully, as well as those aspects of the situation which enable you to perform well and those which cause you problems. For example, how do you perform better: if you structure the task as much as possible, or if you leave it vague and open to discussion? Do you manage better if you talk your plans over with your boss, or if you play your cards close to your vest?

The second argument, that it is a moral responsibility of the leader to tackle every problem which comes along, is a matter of conscience. Is it cowardice to duck when you are asked to do a job you know you can't handle, or is it honesty to refuse responsibilities for which you are not suited by temperament or personality? Unless you try new jobs you will not realize your full potential. If you fail, your career may be in jeopardy and the organization may fail in an important mission.

On the other hand, a general practitioner surely should not undertake open-heart surgery just because he or she would feel bad to duck the challenge. Likewise, a Navy or Army officer who volunteers for an important mission even though he might perform poorly is not doing himself, or his organization, a particular service. There are no simple answers for these problems and you, as every leader, will have to strike the balance which seems best to you in light of your self-knowledge and the leadership situation you face. Whatever you decide to do, it is important that you have as much information as possible to help make an informed choice.

Apply these ideas to the following probe.

➤ **PROBE   23**

Your boss has just called you in to tell you about a job opening at a higher managerial level. She wants to know if you would like to be recommended for the job. Here are the relevant facts:

You are a low LPC leader. For the last four years you have been the Department Head for the tax section of a public accounting firm and feel that you have done especially well in the last two years. The work is challenging but there are clear procedures and guidelines for most of the work.

The new job would require you to take over the entire management of your firm's regional office. This would involve supervising several department heads (e.g., Taxes, Securities, General Auditing), the office staff, as well as meeting the public to secure new business and handle public relations. You recognize that the job is much more unstructured than the one you have now. You also realize, however, that this may represent the only avenue of advancement in the firm.

Should you take the job? There is, of course, no right or wrong answer to this question. The actual choice might depend on many factors which are not discussed above. For example, are you content to stay in your present job and will the organization let you? Do you have any alternative jobs which are appealing to you? What are the effects of failure?

For this exercise, and after considerable thought, let's say that you decide that you want the job. You are going to have another talk with your boss. Knowing her, you think that you can ask for certain conditions under which you would take the new job, but not too many. You have prepared a list of potential things to ask for, and you have decided to ask for three. Your list is shown below. Pick your three most useful actions.

_____ (a)   You want to pick one or two of your past subordinates to work in your new office.

_____ (b)   You want your new office employees to be told that the assignment is for a trial period only and may not be permanent.

_____ (c)   You want a three-month period in the new office to work and learn under the present manager.

_____ (d)   You want to be guaranteed periodic training courses both within the firm and outside.

_____ (e)   You want a free hand in hiring, firing, and transfer.

_____ (f)   You want loose supervision from above.

Feedback is given on the next page.

FEEDBACK ←————————————————————

Assuming that you could request any of the choices, your best bets are (a), (c), and (d). Choice (a) will do much to improve your leader-member relations. You will have some people on whom you can rely and who can help to spread a positive image of you to the employees who are new to you. It is, of course, important that the employees already at the office are not hurt or angered by being displaced.

Another very important step is provided in choice (c). An observation and transition period under the present manager will provide considerable on-the-job training and experience. This should add an important degree of structure to the new job. Along with the training stressed in choice (d), this job should be well along the dimension towards high control. These three measures should facilitate the match between leader and situation.

The other three possible actions have either minimal or undesirable effects. Telling your office staff that the position is temporary, choice (b), would lower your position power; having a free hand in hiring and firing, choice (e), would increase your position power. The effects of increasing power alone, however, are insufficient to move this to a higher area of control. Loose supervision, choice (f) may have a somewhat positive effect in reducing feedback and potential guidance.

SUMMARY

Job engineering means the modification of your leadership situation so that it matches your leadership style. Remember that the typical organization or the typical leadership situation is much more flexible than we usually realize. You can change your relations with subordinates, and your relations with superiors. You may be able to modify the structure of the task as well as the degree to which you use your position power. You can also increase your job knowledge by training and by experience.

Learning how to adjust these factors so that they fit the particular leadership style you bring to the job is perhaps one of the most important means by which you can improve your leadership performance. These same modifications also apply to your subordinate leaders, as we shall discuss in Part IV on "Management of Managers."

PART III SELF-TEST

Listed below are several actions a manager might take to change his situational control. After reading each one, indicate whether you think the action would increase or decrease the leader's situational control.

Increase Control	Decrease Control	
_____	___✓___	1. Frequently volunteer for new and different assignments.
___✓___	_____	2. Ask your superior to let you make all vacation and leave decisions for your subordinates.
___✓___	_____	3. Meet with your boss to set goals and objectives for your department.
_____	___✓___	4. Encourage your subordinates to make suggestions on how to accomplish job-related objectives.
___✓___	_____	5. Get your boss' agreement to bring into your department several subordinates with whom you have worked in the past.
_____	___✓___	6. Avoid close monitoring of your subordinates. Let them work on their own for relatively long periods.
___✓___	_____	7. Keep close records on the effect of various procedures and methods for solving problems or making decisions.
_____	___✓___	8. Volunteer to accept, as subordinates, employees who are trying to transfer out of other departments.

Indicate whether the statements below are true or false.

___F___ 9. Relationship-motivated (high LPC) leaders perform best in low control situations.

___F___ 10. Task-motivated (low LPC) leaders perform best in high and moderate control situations.

_____ _I_____   11.   Low LPC (task-motivated) leaders will behave in a directive, task-focused manner in a low control situation; therefore, their performance will be relatively better than that of high LPC leaders.

_____ _I_____   12.   The relationship-motivated (high LPC) leader will be anxious and tense in a low control situation, performing poorly.

_____ _F_____   13.   The relationship-motivated (high LPC) leader performs best in a high control situation.

Answers to Section III Self-Test

Increase Control	Decrease Control	
_____	__X__	1. *Frequently volunteer for new and different assignments.* By changing jobs frequently, a manager does not build up experience. Thus each new job will present new, unstructured, and challenging problems to the manager.
__X__	_____	2. *Ask your superior to let you make all vacation and leave decisions for your subordinates.* Having the organization give you decision power over such matters increases both your actual power and your subordinates' perception of your authority.
__X__	_____	3. *Meet with your boss to set goals and objectives for your department.* Setting goals and objectives helps to clarify job demands and provides a way to assess performance, thus increasing task structure.
_____	__X__	4. *Encourage your subordinates to make suggestions on how to accomplish job-related objectives.* By asking your subordinates to make suggestions, you are automatically telling them that they have some say in the running of the department. The delegation of authority to subordinates lessens your situational control.
__X__	_____	5. *Get your boss' agreement to bring into your department several subordinates with whom you have worked in the past.* This is a powerful way to improve your leader-member relations. By choosing employees with whom you have had a good working relationship, you increase the support and loyalty of your work group.
_____	__X__	6. *Avoid close monitoring of your subordinates. Let them work on their own for relatively long periods.* When you allow subordinates to work on their own, you increase their authority, and you also make it possible for a diversity of procedures to develop as each subordinate works out his or her own methods. Both of these

Increase Control	Decrease Control	
		factors serve to reduce the leader's control and to increase the challenge of the job.
X	_____	7. *Keep close records on the effect of various procedures and methods for solving problems or making decisions.* Good records provide structure. They allow you to assess which procedures work best and allow you to rely on these procedures for future problems.
_____	X	8. *Volunteer to accept, as subordinates, employees who are trying to transfer out of other departments.* While it may not be true in every case, you will probably receive your share of hard-to-handle employees. This will make the managing of your work group more unpredictable and, therefore, more challenging.*

False   9. *Relationship-motivated (high LPC) leaders do not perform best in low control situations.* The relationship-motivated leader performs best in *moderate* control situations.

False   10. *Task-motivated (low LPC) leaders do not perform best in high and moderate control situations.* While task-motivated leaders do perform well in a high control situation, they perform poorly in the moderate situation. It is important to distinguish between the two.

True   11. *Low LPC (task-motivated) leaders will behave in a directive, task-focused manner in a low control situation; therefore, their performance will be relatively better than that of high LPC leaders.* Task-motivated leaders do perform better than the relationship-motivated leaders in the low control situation. This is usually reflected by their task-oriented behavior.

True   12. *The relationship-motivated (high LPC) leader will be anxious and tense in a low control situation, performing poorly.* In a low control situation, relationship-motivated leaders are anxious

---

* A warning is in order here. We are not suggesting that you try to take on employees who are incompetent or dangerous to the organization. Rather, it is often the case that an employee is somewhat difficult to handle but has promise as an effective worker. For example, frequently in the sports world, an athlete will perform poorly and create dissension on one team, but prove to make a very strong contribution to a new team whose coach is better able to deal with the athlete's needs.

and tense and become so concerned with seeking the support of subordinates that they do poorly at the task at hand.

False   13. *The relationship-motivated (high LPC) leader does not perform best in a high control situation.* The relationship-motivated leader performs best in *moderate* control situations.

By now you should have a good grasp of the things that can increase or decrease a leader's control. Examine your own job and organization and see how many of them are possible for you.

PART IV

Management of Managers

CHAPTER TEN

Engineering the Leadership Situation of Your Subordinates

Up to now we have been primarily concerned with the way in which you can deal with your own leadership job. In this and the following chapter, we want to consider how you can assist your subordinate leaders to perform more effectively since their performance is a reflection of your own leadership.

You may find it relatively easier to modify your subordinates' leadership situations than your own, once you determine the types of situations in which they perform best. The principles are, of course, well known to you by this time: you want to have leadership situations with high or low control for your task-motivated leaders, and leadership situations with moderate control for your relationship-motivated leaders.

As the boss of other leaders, you are in an excellent position to counsel them on the types of leadership situations in which they appear to perform well. You are able to give them not only guidance, but also tangible assistance by modifying their leadership situation. If you desire, you can work with them using the scales and this program to analyze their situation, and determine what is best for them.

There are many different ways in which you can help match your subordinate leaders' job situation with their abilities. You can assign the leader to harmonious or to more conflicting groups, and gradually change the composition of the group to make it more harmonious or more challenging as a problem in personnel administration. You can assign to one leader highly structured tasks, or give highly detailed and specific instructions on how the task is to be accomplished. You can assign to another leader the problems and tasks which are naturally more vague and nebulous, or you can give your instructions in a less specific manner and imply that the leader and his group are to develop their own procedures in dealing with the problem.

You can shore up the leader's authority by providing a great deal of support and backing, by assuring that all the organizational information is channeled through the leader, and by extending greater authority to reward and punish or by letting everyone know that you will almost certainly accept the leader's recommendations.

You can give leaders close emotional support by making yourself available to them for guidance and advice, by being as nonthreatening as possible, and by giving them assurance that you stand behind them. Alternatively, you can take a more aloof, evaluative stance, implying that subordinate leaders are on their own, and that it is up to them to find the right methods and to develop the appropriate policies to deal with their problems. While this latter way of dealing with your subordinate leaders might appear cold, certain types of leaders are better able to perform in this type of climate than in a warmer, more accepting atmosphere. There are also leaders who prefer this type of relationship with their boss. Different types of people perform better under different sorts of control, and we should not automatically assume that our preference is shared by all.

Again, we must stress that you should proceed with care and caution. Small steps in a particular direction will enable you to retrace a wrong approach. Of equal importance, small steps are seen as less threatening since they permit your subordinate leaders to adjust to the changing conditions under which they have to work as you gradually change the amount of control which their leadership situation provides.

SELECTION AND PLACEMENT WITHIN YOUR ORGANIZATION

You can also modify the leadership situation of your subordinate managers by a variety of other methods. One good way is selection and placement, that is, the proper assignment of your subordinates to a leadership situation in which they are most likely to perform well.

Before we go any further, let us stress that we are talking only about leaders who are technically qualified to perform their functions. Nobody should head a team of aircraft designers unless they have had training in engineering, nobody should direct an auditing department unless they have had training in accountancy. In the discussions which follow we are talking about leaders, or candidates for leadership positions, who have at least the minimal basic skills and knowledge which their prospective job requires.

Given the knowledge and skill level of the subordinate, selection and placement are, perhaps, the most obvious methods for improving the subordinate leader's performance. Yet, by and large, our ability to make these assignments has not really been too successful. The well-worn phrase that we must put round pegs into round holes and square pegs into square holes is good advice provided we are dealing with pegs and pegboards which don't change. But organizations *do* change, as do leaders, and so does the relationship of the leader to the position to which he is assigned.

What does this mean for the management strategies you can adopt in selecting and placing the leaders who report to you? The answer depends, of course, on whether you need someone who will perform well immediately or whether you need someone for the long run. It will also depend on how long the "long run" might be. Does it take a few months to become an experienced hand and learn all about the job, or is this a highly complex and difficult task which might take several years to learn? If the latter, then a "short run" strategy is more likely to pay off than waiting several years before your subordinate leader hits his full stride. If, on the other hand, the leadership job can be learned in just a few months, or less than a year, you might be better off to pick someone who might not perform so well at first but who will become very effective within a relatively short time.

Let us say that you have a situation you diagnose as giving potentially *high control* to the experienced leader. This means, as we said earlier, that the job's situational control initially will be only moderate for the new leader. You, therefore, have a choice of selecting a relationship- or task-motivated leader.

If you select a relationship-motivated leader, he or she will perform well at first because relationship-motivated people perform best in *moderate control* situations. However, as the leader gains in experience, the situation moves into the high control condition and the relationship-motivated leader's performance will decrease.

If you select a task-motivated leader, he or she will perform rather poorly at first because task-motivated people do not perform at their best in moderate-control situations. However, as he gains in experience, he will improve and eventually overtake his relationship-motivated counterpart.

The opposite holds true if you initially classify the job as having moderate control for the leader. Until the leader has gained in experience and training, the situation will be low control. Your selection problem now must involve the decision whether to go with the task-motivated leader for immediate results or for the relationship-motivated leader over the long haul. Selection then should reflect short and long-term goals.

Let us look at this problem in graphic form:

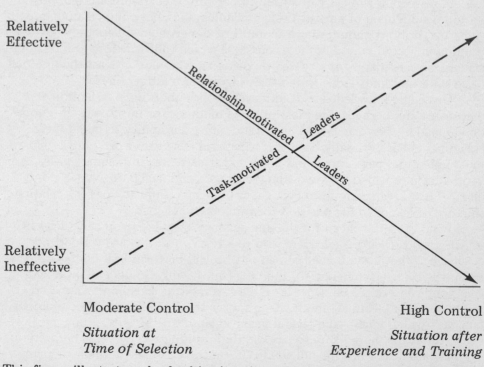

This figure illustrates a leadership situation which is very high in control for the experienced leader, and therefore only moderate for the new leader who has just been assigned to the job. This is shown on the horizontal axis across the bottom. The vertical axis indicates the leader's effectiveness in performing his job, as measured by the effectiveness of his task-group.

The arrows show that the relationship-motivated leader starts off with good performance but gradually becomes less effective. The task-motivated leader starts off rather poorly but becomes more effective as he learns his job.

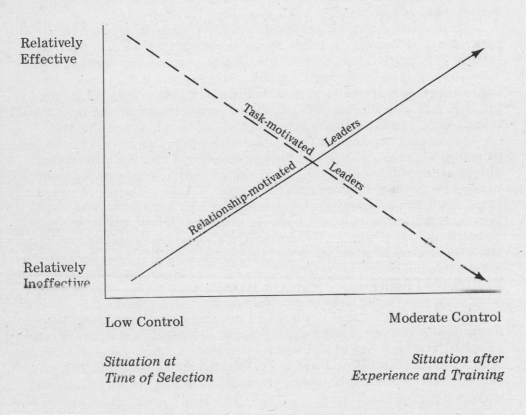

The graph above shows the same basic relationship; but here, the leadership situation is low in control for the new leader but becomes moderate for the experienced and trained leader. Now the task-motivated leader will be more effective immediately while the relationship-motivated leader will perform better later on.

As the manager of subordinate leaders you now have a number of options. Knowing the personality of your subordinates, and the nature of the task, you can select the leader who will excel at the beginning, or the type of leader who will gradually mature into a great performer.

You may require that certain leaders obtain intensive training, knowing that others may perform just as well with little or no training (again remembering that all leaders must have minimum qualifications in order to be considered for a leadership position).

You should insure that leaders are either placed in a position in which they can perform well or that the situation is modified so that their leadership potential is used to the fullest.

Let us now consider the options which are open to you in selecting subordinate leaders for maximum performance.

If you have opted for long range performance, the recommendations which might guide your procedures are indicated in the table on the next page. The general rule is that you wish to keep task-motivated leaders in high control and low control situations or get them there as soon as possible, and relationship-motivated leaders in moderate control situations or get them there as soon as possible.

As the table shows, leaders who are newly assigned or selected for a particular situation will, of course, have less control than the experienced leaders. This means that certain leaders need to be trained or coached, their tasks structured and their position power increased as quickly as possible. Other leaders who are matched to the situation as soon as they are assigned to it will gradually increase their situational control over time and must then be reassigned or rotated to a different job before becoming less effective.

Let us take, for example, a situation which gives high control to the experienced leader (high LMR, high task structure, and high position power). This situation will be only moderate in control for the inexperienced leader whom you are planning to assign. If the leader is task-motivated, you want to get him into the high control situation as quickly as possible. You should, therefore, provide training and coaching, structure his task, give him support and high position power. The relationship-motivated leader will also be in a moderate control situation when you first assign him. You want to keep him in this situation as long as possible. Thus, do not increase his leader control. Eventually you will have to rotate this leader to another job or make his job more complex in order to keep him challenged.

Where you have chosen leaders for immediate, short-run results, the recommendations which might guide your procedures are shown in the table opposite. You must first of all be aware that leaders chosen for short-term results will then not perform well if left too long on the same job. This may be a matter of months or of several years, depending on the job. Suggested strategies might be as follows:

- Do not encourage intensive training which will quickly make the situation higher in control and less challenging, and thus decrease the leader's performance.

- Allow your subordinate leaders to struggle with their problems without becoming over-protective, or giving them a high degree of support. Carefully gauge how much support from you is most desirable to enable them to perform well.

- Consider assigning new personnel periodically to the leader to keep his situation challenging.

Again, it is extremely important that you continually monitor and evaluate the performance of subordinate managers. This will enable you to insure the maximum effectiveness from them and allow you to make adjustments where necessary to maintain the appropriate match for your subordinate managers. Now try the probes beginning on page 182.

If the situation for the experienced leader is:	The situation for the inexperienced leader is:	If the leader is:	To obtain best Long-Range Performance, proceed as follows:	To obtain best Short-Run Performance proceed as follows:
High Control	Moderate Control	Task-motivated	Train leader Structure task Increase position power Support leader	If possible, do not select If selected, train Structure task Provide position power
		Relationship-motivated	Do not increase leader control Rotate eventually	Select if possible Do not train Keep task structure low
Moderate Control	Low Control	Task-motivated	Do not increase leader control	Select if possible Do not train or structure task more than necessary
		Relationship-motivated	Train leader Structure task Support leader Increase position power, to move situation to moderate as quickly as possible	If possible, do not select If selected, train intensively, support, structure task
Low Control	Very Low Control	Task-motivated	Support leader Structure task Increase position power Train leader	Select if possible
		Relationship-motivated		Do not select

───────────────────────────────────➤ **PROBE 24**

You are the manager of the Distribution Division of a large book publishing house and are responsible for all the distribution centers across the country. One of these branches located in a nearby city has been steadily going downhill. Book orders are not processed on time, the billings are frequently mixed up, customers are irate and cancelling orders and two shipping clerks quit in one week. Clearly a new manager must be found as soon as possible. You are told that you can select anyone you like, but that you must produce results as quickly as possible.

In reviewing the situation you have determined that this would be a high control situation for the experienced leader: the manager has a structured task, strong position power, and the employees usually have gotten along well with the manager so that the leader would have maximum control. However, for a *new* leader, the situation initially will be only moderate in control. The new person will have to establish relations with the employees and straighten out the mess left by the previous manager. This may take as long as a year.

After you screen the personnel files and recommendations of all qualified managers who should be considered for the job, you find two serious candidates.

Bill Smith has been with the company for about ten years and has been a line manager in production for about six of these. He is an efficient man who has good employee relations although personally, he is considerate but somewhat distant. He runs an excellent department although when he first came to the department he seemed to have had some trouble with employees who felt that he was pushing them too hard. The division for which he is now being considered is, of course, quite different from Bill Smith's current job.

Jan Jones also arrived in the company some time ago, in fact about the same time as did Bill Smith. She had a reputation as a real winner who did a remarkable job some years ago. Recently there has been some talk that Jones has been resting on her laurels. Her performance and effectiveness leave something to be desired. Her relations with employees, which were very good at first, also have deteriorated somewhat because she is seen as a little bossy and more concerned with how she gets along with her superior than with her subordinates.

Whom would you choose?

_____ (a) Bill Smith because you think he is task-motivated and this is just what you need to straighten out this mess.

_____ (b) Bill Smith because he is relationship-motivated and he will be able to straighten the problems out in time.

_____ (c) Jan Jones because as a task-motivated person she will tend to perform well in a different situation.

_____ (d) Jan Jones because relationship-motivated people perform best in situations of this type.

Turn to the next page for feedback.

FEEDBACK ◄─────────────────────────

(a) **You chose (a):** *Bill Smith because you think he is task-motivated and this is just what you need to straighten out the mess.* This is not correct. While Bill Smith is task-motivated, as you correctly noted, you must remember that task-motivated people in moderate control situations perform well only after they have gained experience. Until they have gained full control, task-motivated people do not perform well. In this case, you must produce results immediately, rather than with someone who will perform well only after he has been there several months or years.

Reread the section on experience on pages 177-181 and try this probe again.

(b) **You chose (b):** *Bill Smith because he is relationship-motivated and he will be able to straighten the problems out in time.* Your choice would indeed be correct if Bill Smith were relationship-motivated. But you will note that Bill Smith was pushing people hard when he first came on the job, that is, when the situation was lower in control. Now that he is in control of the situation he seems quite relaxed and at ease and has good, albeit distant, relations with employees. He also does a good job now in this situation which is surely very high control. These are all marks of the task-motivated leader.

Reread the section describing relationship- and task-motivated people (pages 8-10) again, and then try this probe again.

(c) **You chose (c):** *Jan Jones, because task-motivated people perform well in a difficult situation.* You are correct in your belief that task-motivated leaders perform best in difficult situations, but you missed the boat on two major counts.

1. Jan Jones is not task-motivated. She is likely to be relationship-motivated. Her relations with employees were good at first, and she also performed very well when she started her job, but she has been less effective lately. She has also become less concerned with her leader-member relations. All this points to relationship-motivation rather than task-motivation.

2. Even though the Distribution Division is a mess, this is not a low control situation. As you recall, it is a moderate control situation. A relationship-motivated leader would, of course, perform best under these conditions.

Reread the section on diagnosing the control of situations in Chapter Seven and also the section on diagnosing personality of leaders in Chapter Two. Then make another choice of the alternatives given in Probe 24.

FEEDBACK ←——————————————————

(d)   **You chose (d):** *Jan Jones because relationship-motivated people perform best in situations of this type.*   This is the correct choice. Jan
Jones is a relationship-motivated leader: She performed well at first and then
gradually went downhill as her training and experience made the situation
higher in control. Also, her relationship with her subordinates shows the
pattern typical of a relationship-motivated leader, i.e., when the situation becomes high control the leader becomes less considerate and more aloof from
subordinates. This new job as head of the distribution division is likely to be
a moderate control situation for a new leader. Thus, a relationship-motivated
leader would perform well at first. Jan Jones would seem to be the right person for that job, as you correctly indicated. Go on to Probe 25.

————————————————————————➤ **PROBE 25**

You are an executive of an oil company with many foreign installations. Your company has a contract to build a new base in a remote area of an Arab country. Most project workers will be local Arab personnel with a few American technicians. You must pick someone to head the field team. He will be in charge of the entire operation which involves the construction of an oil exploration and drilling base and the development of procedures to make the base operational. You will be able to give the person you choose some culture training which should give him or her some knowledge of what cultural patterns might affect the work.

You have the following personnel from which to pick your manager. Whom would you choose?

_____ (a) Charles Meecham. An experienced relationship-motivated engineer with specific training in base construction.

_____ (b) Sam Kennedy. A brilliant young task-motivated engineer with very little experience.

_____ (c) Roy Stewart. A bright relationship-motivated engineer. Very little experience.

_____ (d) Nick Foster. A highly experienced task-motivated engineer, trained in base design and maintenance.

Go to the following page for feedback.

FEEDBACK ◄──────────────────────────

This was a difficult item which had many facets and required considerable thought — in other words, a typical leadership problem.

Your first thought should have been to figure out the situational control of the job. Building an oil base in a foreign country with a culturally-mixed work force could not even come close to being a high control situation. It is probably moderate for a trained and experienced man and very low for an untrained person. The cultural training might take some of the conflict out of the culturally mixed group, and improve leader-member relations somewhat. The field manager will have high position power.

Here we threw you another curve. Basing a decision only on the theory presented in this manual, you could choose either the experienced Charles Meecham or the inexperienced Sam Kennedy. While both of these choices fit the theory, (i.e., Meecham is a relationship-motivated leader whose experience makes the situation moderate in control, and Kennedy, a task-motivated leader whose lack of experience makes the situation low in control.), they are obviously not equally good in practice. One must feel extremely hesitant to send a young and inexperienced person on such a difficult job. Charles Meecham is, therefore, the better choice.

This exercise helps to illustrate an important point made in the introduction. This program will augment sound management thinking, not replace it. An executive would surely want to send a trained and experienced person to head an important project in the field. The method detailed here helps the executive select which person is likely to have the most effective leadership pattern.

---→ **PROBE 26**

Tom Fleming is a young civil engineer who was recently hired as a first line supervisor in your department and he is still quite inexperienced. Tom came very highly recommended, is highly intelligent, and very well motivated. You place him in charge of a construction crew to build a typical logging road into a wilderness area. While the men seem to like him moderately well, his performance has been quite disappointing and his crew is behind schedule. When the work is not going too well (which has happened quite a lot lately) he more or less locks himself into his office and works on new plans and procedures and he spends very little time with his men.

You need to take some action to remedy the situation to see if his performance can be improved. Tom's LPC score is 44. He has been on the job about six months and he still seems very nervous about doing well. The company has no special training program for this rough (but quite routine) kind of road building. You have listed below several possible actions which you might take. Check the best course or courses of action.

_____ (a) Tell Tom that his performance is poor and give him a reasonable time period (say three months) to improve performance or be replaced.

_____ (b) Introduce Tom to one of the older, more experienced supervisors and ask this person to give him a few pointers.

_____ (c) Sit down with Tom and try to plan out some short range goals and some guidelines for building logging roads. This should improve his task structure somewhat.

_____ (d) Give Tom a new assignment with a chance to demonstrate how creative he can be.

_____ (e) Suggest to Tom that he spend more time getting to know his crew and gaining their support and confidence.

Turn to the next page for feedback.

FEEDBACK ◄──────────────────────────

Choices (b), (c) and (e) represent possible solutions to Tom's problem. Tom is a low LPC, or task-motivated, leader. He is new to the job and probably does not yet know and understand exactly what to do. Thus, the situation is moderate in control. Tom is probably pressing too hard and performing poorly. The best course of action involves taking steps to increase his control of the situation until it better matches Tom's leadership style.

Choices (b) and (c) both involve increasing task structure. In one case this is done through informal training by an experienced person and in the other by providing task structure from his superior. Increasing structure is probably not enough by itself to move his job into a higher zone. So choice (e) perhaps in combination with (c) may be the best selection because it involves leader-member relations which is the most important dimension. Changing *both* leader-member relations and task structure, however, should definitely improve Tom's situation.

Choices (a) and (d) both involve decreasing control by adding stress or decreasing task structure. Neither course of action is warranted. It is true that the situation could change enough to become a low-control situation, and that Tom's performance might improve somewhat. As we have said earlier, however, this is a dangerous and potentially poor course of action. Very low control situations often tend to be quite volatile and do not represent a stable, productive situation.

Be sure to re-evaluate situations of this type in a few weeks to see if your changes have improved the leader's performance.

If you got this one right — you're on your way! Now try Probe 27.

If you missed this one, you should review Chapter Three on determining situational control.

────────────────────────────────► **PROBE 27**

You are the President of an architectural engineering firm. You have recently hired a young engineer, Jack Meyer, to direct the bridge design section of
your firm. He is a brilliant young man who should be a strong addition to
your firm. He is a low LPC leader.

Meyer's job as head of the bridge section is to direct the work of several engineers and draftsmen who design or draft portions of larger projects.
The work of his subordinates is reasonably well structured. They work within specifiable limits with fairly standard procedures. Several of these men are
older and more experienced but less talented than their leader. They like him
well enough but are not really sure that he should be their boss.

Your problem is that Meyer's department performance has been relatively poor and is costing the company money in terms of overtime and pen-
alties. In addition, he has been using strong discipline to get the department
moving. This does not work very well, especially since company structure
gives the section leader no real power to hire or fire people. Authority for
hiring as well as salaries and promotion are centered in the personnel department and higher management levels. The situational control is likely to be
moderate.

Listed below are the courses of action which might have the effect of
improving the performance of the bridge department. Choose those which
you think are most appropriate to the present situation.

_____ (a) Change the personnel of his unit so that it will be more difficult
for him to get to know his staff.

_____ (b) Start taking actions designed to improve Meyer's authority and
position, e.g., channel all information through him, include him in
meetings at higher levels, make it clear that his suggestions carry
weight.

_____ (c) Provide Meyer with intensive training and guidance.

_____ (d) Transfer him to a new job, and keep moving him around so that
his job remains exciting and challenging.

_____ (e) Fire him. His performance indicates that the high expectations for
him were in error.

_____ (f) Leave him alone. Things will probably get better eventually.

_____ (g) Allow him to add a couple of men of his own choice to his department.

The next page will give you feedback on your choices.

FEEDBACK ←

Jack Meyer is in a moderate control situation, a position appropriate for a high LPC leader. Meyer is, however, a low LPC leader, and therein lies the problem.

An evaluation of various alternatives is given below:

(a) *Change the personnel of his unit so it will be more difficult for him to get to know his staff.* This might lower the situational control to an area which is more suitable for a low LPC leader. This course of action would probably be unwise for two reasons. First, it is in general a bad idea to push a leadership situation into low control regardless of leadership style. Groups in such a situation frequently show a general decrease in performance. Second, as Meyer became more experienced the structure of his job would increase, carrying him back into an inappropriate level of situational control.

(b) *Start taking actions designed to improve Meyer's authority and position.* This would be a useful but not a sufficient course of action. Improving his power would move the situation closer to high control. However, since power is the weakest of the three situational dimensions, this action alone would probably not be enough.

(c) *Provide Meyer with intensive training and guidance.* This would be a good course of action. Providing him with training would have the same effect as giving him a more structured task. This would be a major step in moving his situation into a high control zone, best suited to his leadership orientation.

(d) *Transfer him to a new job.* This action is contraindicated. Moving him around would have the effect of maintaining an unstructured and ambiguous task environment which is the last thing he needs.

(e) *Fire him.* This action would be premature. From what we know about situational effects on leadership performance, it would be unwise to dismiss a talented and potentially useful manager without attempting to salvage his talents.

(f) *Leave.him alone.* This is a possible option. Experience and stability will eventually improve the situation enough to improve Meyer's performance. However, the company probably cannot afford to wait that long.

(g) *Allow him to choose some new subordinates.* This would be a positive step. It would allow Meyer to improve the support of his subordinates by bringing in some people he can work with, and possibly showing others that he can be a good man for whom to work. This could also backfire, causing further alienation among his subordinates in the bridge department.

SUMMARY

This chapter dealt with engineering your managers' jobs, and with leadership selection and placement, stressing that the control of the situation changes as the leader gains in experience on a particular job. Therefore, we cannot merely place a task-motivated leader in high control or low control situations, and a relationship-motivated leader in a moderate control situation. Rather, we must consider that new leaders will experience the situation as lower in control until they have established themselves as trustworthy with their group members, and until they have learned the task fully.

The time it takes for a leader to reach his full level of experience will vary according to the job. Leaders who are assigned to relatively simple tasks will take less time than those who are assigned to very complex and difficult tasks. Leaders who are given extensive training will take less time than those who are untrained. And leaders assigned to "difficult" groups will take longer to develop good leader-member relations (if they can do so at all) than will leaders who are assigned to congenial, highly homogeneous groups.

Sound strategy calls for the selection and placement of leaders by long-run or short-run needs. Choose leaders whose best performance is required immediately but who can be expected to become less effective over time, or leaders who may perform rather poorly at first but who will become increasingly better as the situation begins to match their personality.

The basic strategies for various conditions of situational control are shown in the table on page 181.

Chapter Eleven describes how to apply these concepts to rotation and transfer.

You can assign a leader to a group that will present a challenge.

CHAPTER ELEVEN

Rotation and Transfer

Moving from one job to another is part of organizational life in many large businesses and industrial concerns as well as in the military services. If these moves are made as particular jobs need to be filled, and if they benefit the organization, they are usually called transfers. When these moves are part of a systematic policy which calls for periodic reassignments to broaden the leader's experience and perspective, they are considered part of a rotation program.

Whatever the reasons for moving, very few managers in large companies, or leaders in the military services, remain in the same position for more than a few years. Until very recently almost nothing was known about the effects which rotation and transfer might have on the effectiveness of the individual or of his organizational unit. The general assumption has been that it must be good for the organization and for the leader since it develops managers with broad perspectives who provide cross-fertilization. Whether it is good for everyone and under all conditions is another question.

Let us here consider the effects of transfers and rotation in light of this training program. What are the likely results of changing jobs, and of high turnover of one's own superiors or subordinates?

While managerial rotation is generally seen as beneficial, "organizational turbulence," (that is, unsystematic turnover among subordinates, changes in job requirement, changes in higher managers, and economic upheaval) is seen as disruptive and as leading to poorer performance. Upon closer inspection, the factors which affect leaders in their day-to-day interactions with their boss, subordinates and peers are identical, whether we talk about rotation, transfer, promotion, or turbulence. In each of these cases leaders must learn to adjust to major changes in their situation.

What specific elements change? A change of boss requires leaders to learn the new superior's standards and expectations, including any idiosyncracies that must be considered. However, the leader and new boss finally adjust to one another. This may take a few months to a few years, and the leader must live with a certain amount of anxiety and insecurity until he or she has gotten to know how to handle the new boss.

Similarly, for a certain amount of time newly-transferred leaders will not be able to trust their new subordinates. Do they really know what they are doing? Can they be relied upon to do the job right? If the leader gets into trouble, will they support him? Who, in the group, are the key people to work with in changing attitudes or morale? All of these questions must be answered before the situation stabilizes.

Finally, leaders must learn what the new job is all about. What must they know about the work itself? How is it done in the new place, how do they look for problems, how do they get things fixed, who are the experts in the organization on whom they must depend, and to whom should they turn for help? Whom should they see if they run into trouble with suppliers, with customers, or with other managers at the same level of organization? Above all, who are the real powers, the people to see if you want to get something done?

These are all important questions whether or not the move was made for the purposes of rotation or promotion, or whether the effects came about because of so-called organizational turbulence. Practically all of these questions lower the leader's control. The major exception is a move by a leader from a low control situation to a new job which involves more control e.g., from being the disliked manager of an advertising department to a well-liked director of a production department.

Since most rotations and transfers change the situation, these moves should correspondingly improve the performance of some leaders but decrease the performance of others.

Staying on the same job too long results in lower performance on the part of some people. They become stale or bored with the job, no longer interested and challenged by the problems they must tackle, and no longer as motivated as they were at first. Others, however, will like the continuity, and they see their constant improvement as a challenge of a different sort. Different people obviously have different strengths and weaknesses as managers.

Consider, for example, your best managerial troubleshooter who is sent out to solve problems. If you leave this person at the same branch office or trouble-spot so long that there are no more fires to extinguish or problems to solve, he or she is likely to become bored and disinterested. There is no more challenge and he or she will now either stir up trouble — which you don't need — or pay less attention to the job and become correspondingly less effective.

Others simply need more time to become maximally effective. They take pride in learning their job inside-out. And some managers are cut out for the day-to-day administration of departments or plants, and do this superbly. But these same people frequently are less able to handle conflict. Therefore, rotation and transfer should take into consideration the individual's leadership style as well as situational control if the effectiveness and the performance of the organizational unit is important.

THE BEST TIME TO ROTATE OR TRANSFER

In principle, the best time comes when the high LPC leader, by virtue of his experience and training, is no longer working in a moderate control situation, or the low LPC leader is no longer working in a high or low control situation. Accurate diagnosis is essential here. You must know not only the personality and leadership style of your subordinate leaders, but also the amount of control of the situation. However, you must also maintain a careful record of leader performance. When the performance of a leader or manager begins to slip, even though the person did an excellent job earlier, then it is time to consider whether the job has become too routine or too structured, and the job has become no longer challenging enough to meet the leader's needs. Then you must decide whether to attempt to engineer the job as we discussed earlier, or if that isn't possible, to rotate or transfer.

In general terms, it will be useful for you to collect information about the relationship of time on the job to the amount of situational control for all the positions under your direction. In some cases, where little information is available, you will have to make an educated guess. Based on your knowledge of the job, you might be able to make a rough estimate of the amount of time it takes to move a position from one area of control to the next as a result of experience.

Your informal observation will usually tell you a good deal. How many months or years does it take until a person in a particular leadership job is no longer considered "new" or "inexperienced"? When does she become "an old hand", that is, someone to whom others turn for advice? You might also ask how long the average manager or leader remains in a particular job. Institutional wisdom and practice frequently are a good indicator as to the peak effectiveness of a managerial job. Thus, if most managers remain at the division manager level for four years before being moved up or out, the optimum time of managerial experience is likely to be around two or three years, with some of the managers becoming notably restless and less effective and others beginning to hit their stride.

A more systematic way to gauge this may be possible. If, for example, a number of leaders have similar positions but varying job tenure, you could have them fill out the rating forms for the positions. From the derived situational control scores you may then be able to observe a trend in situational changes.

In all of these procedures, you are trying to find out about how long it takes to increase leader control in a particular situation. That information will allow you to make a better decision on whom to rotate or transfer from one job to another, and when.

Whether you make a systematic survey or only an educated guess, there is no substitute for carefully maintained performance evaluations, or whenever possible, carefully kept objective measures of performance. We cannot overemphasize the point that good performance records and evaluations are valuable assets for any organization that wants to develop and keep a well performing pool of leadership and managerial talent.

Now try the probe on the following page.

→ **PROBE 28**

You are the general manager of an assembly plant. Company policy requires the periodic rotation of managers, generally every four years. However, you know that certain people need longer, others less time to reach their maximum performance levels.

Tim Caldwell, one of your division managers, has been on the job for 17 months. The division he heads deals with engineering and maintenance problems, a highly structured task. Caldwell started off very well. His relations with his men were excellent, he was enthusiastic about the job, and he liked to tackle new problems. He is known as an approachable and sociable person. Several months ago his relations with his men began to deteriorate. You have the feeling that he is trying to impress you, and that he is no longer involved with the work itself.

How would you diagnose the problem?

(a)   Caldwell is a low LPC person who needs to be transferred to a new job which is more highly structured.

(b)   Caldwell is a high LPC person, and what you see is simply the consequence of his "moving" from a moderate control to a high control situation. You therefore rotate him to a new job of moderate control.

(c)   Caldwell is low LPC. His situation was low in control to begin with, and it has become moderate. He therefore needs another low control situation, and you plan to change his job to that of troubleshooter for the design section.

(d)   Caldwell is high LPC, and you decide that he needs to remain on the job until he gets his feet back on the ground. You figure that he would do best if you gave him a smaller unit since he is good at supervising this type of work.

FEEDBACK ←

(a) You chose (a): *Caldwell is a low LPC person who needs to be transferred to a new job which is more highly structured.* This is incorrect. All indications are that you are dealing with a high LPC person, and his good performance at the beginning of his job as well as his good relations with subordinates at that time point to this conclusion. Likewise, the fact that Caldwell is trying to develop good relations with you rather than with his subordinates is characteristic of a high LPC leader in a high control situation. Remember that the high LPC leaders become inconsiderate of their subordinates if the situation is too high in control. Caldwell's situation appears to be high control now that he had been on the job for quite some time. He has position power, and he has a structured task. His relations with his subordinates are fairly good although perhaps not quite as good as they were at the beginning.

You missed on this one. Review the first few chapters and then try this probe again.

(b) You chose (b): *Caldwell is a high LPC person, and what you see is simply the consequence of his "moving" from a moderate control to a high control situation. You therefore rotate him to a new job of moderate control.* This is correct on both counts. You should rotate Caldwell to a situation which is moderate control for a new leader. This might well be a task which, after an appropriate time interval, might become high in control. But for the moment, you are best off with Caldwell in a job which challenges him. It would probably be unwise to assign him to a job which is unstructured, has low position power and possibly poor leader-member relations (that is, a situation which is likely to be low in control), in the expectation that he will in time and with experience have a moderate control leadership situation. You are better off to consider him for a job which is moderate in control right now.

(c) You chose (c): *Caldwell is a low LPC. His situation was low in control to begin with, and it has become moderate. He, therefore, needs another low control situation and you plan to change his job to that of troubleshooter for the design section.* This is not correct. The brief description of Caldwell's relations with his subordinates indicates that he is probably a high LPC person. He was friendly and approachable at first, but his relationships deteriorated over time and he began to seek a closer relationship with the boss. This is a pattern typical of high LPC persons.

FEEDBACK ◄────────────────────────

Note also that he deals with a highly structured task. It is unlikely that this situation was ever low in control. It was probably of moderate control for a new leader and became high in control as the leader gained experience.
Rethink this probe and make another choice.

(d)   **You chose (d):** *Caldwell is high LPC, and you decide that he needs to remain on the job until he gets his feet back on the ground. You figure that he would do best if you gave him a smaller unit since he is good at supervising this type of work.* We have some good news and some bad news. The good news is that you accurately assessed Caldwell's leadership style. The bad news is that your plan of action is likely to make his performance even worse.

Caldwell's problem appears to stem from the fact that with experience his job has become too structured, and he has lost interest and motivation. The solution is not to increase his control further, as would be the result if you leave him on the same job and give him responsibilities which are very structured. Rather, he should be given a job which better suits his leadership motivation, that is, less structured.

Consider the alternatives, and make another choice.

SUMMARY

Leadership situations change over time as do the knowledge and abilities which a leader brings to a task. As the leader gains in experience, ability, and job knowledge, each leadership assignment will become more routine and less challenging.

One important method for increasing the challenge of the job involves decreasing the leader's situational control by systematic rotation of the manager to another job. Keeping good performance records will help you to judge the most appropriate time for rotating or transferring a subordinate leader.

Now try the Part IV Self-Test on the next page.

PART IV SELF-TEST

Select the statement that best completes or answers each item below.

_____ 1. The largest and most dramatic changes in engineering leadership situations for subordinates will result from actions affecting:

(a) Leader-member relations

(b) Task structure

(c) Position power

(d) Overall situational control

_____ 2. You are selecting a manager to direct the operation of a bookkeeping department with fairly routine procedures and responsibilities. Leader-member relations should be quite good, and position power is high. You need immediate performance at a high level. What type of leader would you select?

(a) Low LPC, task-motivated

(b) High LPC, relationship-motivated

_____ 3. You are selecting a manager for your firm's extensive public relations functions. Morale is good, but the job is extremely unstructured. You are primarily concerned with high level performance over the long run. What type of leader would you choose?

(a) Low LPC, task-motivated

(b) High LPC, relationship-motivated

_____ 4. The effect of job rotation on situational control is:

(a) Generally to increase control

(b) Generally to decrease control

(c) Generally to not affect control

_____ 5. You have a subordinate manager who is a low LPC, task-motivated leader. She is presently in a situation of moderate control and is performing poorly. Which of the following courses of action is best?

(a) Increase the pressure on her, tighten deadlines, and become personally aloof.

(b) Provide her with better guidelines, more frequent feedback, and a better feeling of support from the organization.

(c) Assign the manager to some extensive training courses, while

you withdraw, become more aloof, and demand higher
performance.

(d)   Do nothing.

Feedback — Part IV Self-Test

__(a)__   1. *The largest and most dramatic changes in engineering leadership
situations for subordinates will result from actions affecting:*
Leader-member relations. Leader-member relations are the single
most important factor affecting the leader's control. Changes in
group composition or in organizational support for the leader can
drastically change the leader's situational control.

__(b)__   2. *You are selecting a manager to direct the operation of a bookkeeping department with fairly routine procedures and responsibilities.
You need immediate performance at a high level. What type of
leader would you select?* High LPC, relationship-motivated. This
situation has the potential to be fairly highly structured. However,
it would be relatively low in structure for a new leader. Assuming
leader-member relations to be reasonably positive, this position is
likely to be of moderate situational control for the new manager.
A high LPC leader should deliver high performance in the short
run.

__(b)__   3. *You are selecting a manager for your firm's extensive public relations functions. Morale is good, but the job is extremely unstructured. You are primarily concerned with high level performance
over the long run. What type of leader would you choose?* High
LPC, relationship-motivated. In this question you must be sensitive
to the long run potential for structure and control. Given the
extremely unstructured nature of public relations, even extensive
time on the job should not make the task very structured. Thus,
even in the long run, the job promises to be one of moderate control calling for a relationship-motivated person.

__(b)__   4. *The effect of job rotation on situational control is:* Generally to
decrease control. Job rotation is a systematic change in leadership
positions. The high rate of change makes it impossible to gain
experience which would add structure and control. Thus, by
restricting opportunities to gain experience, rotation effectively
decreases control.

__(b)__   5. *You have a subordinate manager who is a low LPC, task-motivated
leader. She is presently in a situation of moderate control and is
performing poorly. Which of the following courses of action is
best?* Provide her with better guidelines, more frequent feedback,

and a better feeling of support from the organization. In a situation like this, as the managers' superior, you want to move her into a zone of maximum control. Choice (b) involves several activities designed to increase control. Choice (a) will lower control. This might put the leader into a very low control situation. This is a dangerous course of action, even for a low LPC leader. Choice (c) is a mixture of contradictory activities and choice (d) relies only on the effects of experience (a relatively slow process) to improve situational control.

CHAPTER TWELVE

A Final Note

You have now completed this training program which is designed to make you a more effective leader. If you have successfully worked through all the exercises and probes, you should have a fairly good understanding of the principles which will enable you to manage your groups more productively.

Let's review a few points which are essential if your leadership performance is to improve and to remain high.

First, this manual has been concerned with effective leadership. Management and leadership involve many other functions, although the direction and supervision of others is the single most important task. Leaders must also counsel their subordinates, they must provide a climate in which their subordinates can grow in professional skills, and they must try to develop a satisfied group which is motivated to work toward the common goal. This requires human relations skills with which we have not dealt in this manual. You may or may not feel the need of training in these areas. Having a satisfied work group is not necessarily related to good performance, but it is a goal to which we should aspire for its own sake, as well as for the sake of those who work with us.

Second, this program is designed to introduce you to a set of principles. It is not designed to be a rule book to which you can turn for specific answers to every problem. This manual can make you aware of factors determining success or failure in a leadership situation. It provides you with ground rules for changing your leadership situation so that your chances for success are improved. It does not guarantee success. There is no substitute for sound judgment, and an attempt to apply the principles of this program uncritically to every problem which you face in your leadership job is almost certain to bring frustration and disappointment. When you learned to swim you were not told how to jump into the Kansas City Municipal pool or how to swim on Waikiki beach. When you were taught to write, you were not given specific instructions on how to write to Aunt Edna or Cousin Ebenezer. You were instructed in the principles which, after practice, allowed you to swim any place, or to write to anyone.

Similarly, you should not expect to find exact answers to your leadership problems in this program. You will need to practice what you have learned and observe how well, given your particular leadership style, the various principles and guidelines apply to your particular situation. You will have to try out a variety of methods before you finally find the ones which seem to work best for you.

Third, leadership is an extremely complex relationship, and many factors determine how well a particular group operates at any one time. You, as a leader, cannot expect to control all of the many things which affect the performance of your group. You cannot singlehandedly change the state of the economy, your organization's market, the favor or disfavor with which the powers-that-be regard your organization or your superiors, nor, in many cases, the types of people who are assigned to you as subordinates.

However, an organization which gives you a good evaluation of your own, and your group's performance, allows you to become aware of the situations and the conditions under which you perform best. Seek out these evaluations, or develop good performance criteria, so that you can monitor and continually improve your leadership skills as well as your ability to seek and develop situations in which you are most likely to succeed.

You can reasonably expect your group's performance to increase considerably when the situation matches your personality and you can hope that your new skills will increase the number of times that you can *make* this happen. And if you can improve the number of times your group performs better, you will, indeed, be way ahead of the game.

*This program is not a rule book to which you
can turn for specific answers to every problem.*

Final Test

The following questions are designed to test your overall understanding of the material presented in this book. Select the statement that best completes or answers each item. Feedback is given following the test.

_____ 1. Relationship-motivated leaders perform best in which of the following:

    (a) Low control situations

    (b) High control situations

    (c) Moderate control situations

    (d) All of the above

_____ 2. The concept of a leadership style is best summarized by:

    (a) A variable, changing, almost random set of attitudes and behaviors.

    (b) A set of personality traits which are associated with effective leadership.

    (c) A motivational pattern or set of needs which the leader seeks to satisfy in the group-task situation.

    (d) A basic behavioral pattern, such as giving orders or asking for suggestions, which the leader shows in _every_ situation.

_____ 3. A structured task is one in which:

    (a) It is difficult to determine whether the job was done right.

    (b) The goal or outcome is clearly stated or known.

    (c) There are many ways to accomplish the task.

    (d) There are many possible solutions.

_____ 4. Three variables are used to specify the situational control of a leadership position. These variables differ in importance. Which choice gives these three variables in their correct order of importance?

    (a) 1. leader-member relations   (b) 1. position power
              2. task structure   2. task structure
              3. position power   3. leader-member relations

(c)   1. task structure   (d) 1. position power
        2. leader-member relations   2. leader-member relations
        3. position power   3. task structure

_____ 5. Much discussion in this program focused on methods of changing situational control. Why weren't methods of changing LPC scores discussed?

    (a)   No one knows what LPC is.

    (b)   Only high LPC persons can change their LPC score.

    (c)   Only low LPC persons can change their LPC score.

    (d)   The LPC score is a measure of stable traits that are difficult to change.

_____ 6. A manager displays the following set of behaviors: Under some stress or uncertainty in his job, he tends to seek out the support and advice of his followers. He avoids conflict and tries to create a warm interpersonal environment. He is not often punitive. He is excited by diverse and challenging problems and performs very well in such situations but becomes aloof, apathetic, and somewhat self-centered when problems and complexity are not present. This manager is likely to be a:

    (a)   High LPC leader (relationship-motivated)

    (b)   Low LPC leader (task-motivated)

    (c)   He does not fit clearly into either of the above categories.

_____ 7. If you were asked to summarize briefly the most important aspect of a leadership situation for leaders, which of the concepts below would be most useful in classifying situations?

    (a)   The degree to which the situation allows leaders to predict with certainty the effects of their behavior.

    (b)   The degree to which leaders feel attracted to their subordinates and co-workers.

    (c)   The degree to which the situation gives the leader formal power over his subordinates.

    (d)   The potential amount of tangible rewards available to the leader and his group.

_____ 8. Leaders and managers often vary in the amount of job-related training and experience which they have. This is thought to be an important aspect of leadership. What is the impact of training and experience? (Choices are given at the top of the next page.)

    (a) Generally, training and experience make a leader more task-oriented, especially more structuring and directive.

    (b) Experience and to a lesser extent, training, tend to improve markedly the performance of most leaders.

    (c) Training and experience generally make the task more structured, thereby improving situational control.

    (d) Training and experience usually make a leader more sensitive to the needs of his or her followers.

_____ 9. If you had a job in which the leader's situation tended to be very good in terms of support from followers, clarity of job demands, and the leader's formal and informal influence, which of the following leader types would be likely to perform best?

    (a) Task-motivated

    (b) Relationship-motivated

    (c) Either of the above

_____ 10. Consider the situation described in the previous question (#9). Now assume that there were major changes in personnel which reduced the group's support of the leader and created group conflict and dissension. What type of leader would be likely to perform best?

    (a) Task-motivated

    (b) Relationship-motivated

    (c) Either of the above

_____ 11. If you wish to increase situational control for a leader, which of the following courses of action would be *most* effective?

    (a) Give the leader a more complex task with fewer guidelines.

    (b) Allow the leader to decide who gets salary bonuses among his subordinates.

    (c) Give the leader a title and greater authority.

    (d) Allow the leader to choose his own subordinates from available personnel.

_____ 12. You have a leadership situation with the following characteristics: Leader-member relations are quite good and position power is moderate to high. The task has a reasonably high degree of structure but is quite complicated and requires the leader to learn quite a bit about it. The situational control of this position is likely to be: (Choices are given at the top of the next page.)

(a) Moderate for an inexperienced leader; high for an experienced leader

(b) Low for an inexperienced leader; high for an experienced leader

(c) Low for an inexperienced leader; moderate for an experienced leader

(d) High for an inexperienced leader; moderate for an experienced leader

_____ 13. Which of the following organizational procedures is likely to decrease situational control for the organization's leaders?

(a) Channeling all relevant organizational information through group leaders

(b) Allowing supervisors and managers to pick their own staffs

(c) A general policy of rotation

(d) A broad program of supervisory and managerial training

_____ 14. The degree of control that a situation presents for the leader can be changed by modifying various aspects of the situation. Which of the following aspects, if changed, will have the most drastic effect on situational control?

(a) Position power

(b) Task structure

(c) Leader-member relations

FEEDBACK ←————————————————————

___c___ 1. *Relationship-motivated leaders perform best in:* Moderate control situations. Task-motivated leaders perform best in high control and low control situations. (See Chapter Eight for review.)

___c___ 2. *The concept of a leadership style is best summarized by:* A motivational pattern or set of needs which the leader seeks to satisfy in the group-task situation. Leadership style is a measure of the individual's motivational pattern and a measure of what goals in the work situation are important to them. If leadership style were a changing, random set of behaviors, this program would not be possible. (See Chapter Two for review.)

___b___ 3. *A structured task is one in which:* The goal or outcome is clearly stated or known. This is the only choice which reflects a structured task. The other answers describe unstructured tasks. (See Chapter Five for review.)

___a___ 4. *Three variables are used to specify the situational control of a leadership position. These variables differ in importance. These variables in their correct order of importance are:* 1. Leader-member relations; 2. task structure; and, 3. position power. Leader-member relations are twice as important as task structure which is twice as important as position power. These weightings are reflected in the various scales which measure situational control; leader-member relations is worth forty points, task structure is worth twenty points, and position power is worth ten points. (See Chapter Seven for review.)

___d___ 5. *Much discussion in this program focused on methods of changing situational control. Methods of changing LPC scores were not discussed because:* The LPC score is a measure of stable traits that are difficult to change. LPC is a reflection of your personality and your basic leadership style. It is nearly impossible to change your personality. However, it is fairly simple to change various aspects of your leadership situation. (See Chapters Two and Nine for review.)

___a___ 6. *A manager displays the following set of behaviors: Under some stress or uncertainty in his job, he tends to seek out the support and advice of his followers. He avoids conflict and tries to create a warm interpersonal environment. He is not often punitive. He is excited by diverse and challenging problems and performs very*

FEEDBACK ←─────────────────────────────

well in such situations, but becomes aloof, apathetic, and some-
what self-centered when problems and complexity are not pres-
ent. This manager is likely to be a: High LPC leader (relationship-motivated). This is an accurate description of the high LPC
(relationship-motivated) leader. If you missed this one, review
the descriptions of the two kinds of leadership styles in Chapter
Two.

a 7. *If you were asked to summarize briefly the most important as-*
pect of a leadership situation for leaders, the concept that
would be most useful in classifying situations is: The degree to
which the situation allows leaders to predict with certainty the
effects of their behavior. If leaders have high situational control,
they can predict with certainty the outcome of their own and
their group's behavior. This is the most important aspect of a
situation for leaders. However, this should not be confused with
choice (b) which is similar to leader-member relations -- the
most important dimension in measuring situational control.
(See Chapter Three for review.)

c 8. *Leaders and managers often vary in the amount of job-related*
training and experience which they have. This is thought to be
an important aspect of leadership. The impact of training and
experience is: Training and experience generally make the task
more structured, thereby improving situational control. Experience and training will tend to improve the performance of some
types of leaders. However, the best answer is that experience
and training have the effect of making the task more structured
for leaders, thereby increasing their control of the situation,
which may, or may not, improve their performance. (See Chapter Five for review.)

a 9. *If you had a job in which the leader's situation tended to be very*
good in terms of support from followers, clarity of job demands,
and the leader's formal and informal influence, the leader type
that would perform best would be: Task motivated. The situation described here is one of high control which is best suited
for the task-motivated leader. (See Chapter Eight for review.)

b 10. *Consider the situation described in the previous question (#9).*
Now assume that there were major changes in personnel which
reduced the group's support of the leader and created group

FEEDBACK ◄───────────────────

conflict and dissension. The type of leader who would be likely to perform best is: Relationship-motivated. Because the leader-member relations are now poor, but with high task structure and position power, the situational control is moderate. The relationship-motivated leader performs best in this type of situation. (See Chapter Eight for review.)

___d___ 11. *If you wish to increase situational control for a leader, the course of action most effective would be:* Allow the leader to choose his own subordinates from available personnel. Because leader-member relations are the most important dimension in determining situational control, allowing the leader to choose his own subordinates from available personnel will increase his leader-member relations, thereby increasing his situational control. Choices (b) and (c) would also improve situational control, but not as much as a change in leader-member relations. (See Chapter Nine for review.)

___a___ 12. *You have a leadership situation with the following characteristics: Leader-member relations are quite good and position power is moderate to high. The task has a reasonably high degree of structure, but it is quite complicated and requires the leader to learn quite a bit about it. The situational control of this position is likely to be:* Moderate for an inexperienced leader; high for an experienced leader. The situation described here is one of high control for an experienced leader, but only moderate in control for the new leader. After the new leader has been on the job for quite some time, the situation will become high in control. (See Chapters Nine and Ten for review.)

___c___ 13. *The organizational procedure most likely to decrease situational control for the organization's leaders is:* A general policy of rotation. A system of general rotation is an effective way to decrease situational control within an organization. Choices (a), (b), and (d) have the effect of increasing situational control. (See Chapters Nine and Ten for review.)

___c___ 14. *The degree of control that a situation presents for the leader can be changed by modifying various aspects of the situation. The most drastic effect on situational control will result from a change in:* Leader-member relations. A change in leader-member relations will have the most effect on situational control. This is because leader-member relations are the most important dimension of situational control and worth more weight in measuring situations. (See Chapters Three, Four, and Nine for review.)

Leader Match Summary

This is a short review of the terms and concepts presented in this book.

First, there are two different kinds of leadership styles which are measured by the Least Preferred Co-worker (LPC) scale.

1. *Relationship-motivated* (high LPC, score of 64 or above) leaders tend to be most concerned with maintaining good interpersonal relations, sometimes even to the point of letting the task suffer. In relaxed and well-controlled situations, this type of person tends to reverse his or her behavior and become more task conscious.

2. *Task-motivated* (low LPC, score of 57 or below) leaders place primary emphasis on task performance. These leaders are the no-nonsense people who tend to work best from guidelines and specific directions. If these are lacking, their first priority is to organize and create these guidelines and then assign the various duties to their subordinates. However, under relaxed and well-controlled situations, task-motivated leaders take the time to be pleasant and pay more attention to the morale of their employees.

Leaders whose score falls between 58 and 63 will have to determine for themselves which category they most nearly resemble.

Second, there are three kinds of leadership situations:

1. *High control* situations allow the leader a great deal of control and influence and a predictable environment in which to direct the work of others.

2. *Moderate control* situations present the leader with mixed problems — either good relations with subordinates but an unstructured task and low position power, or the reverse, poor relations with group members but a structured task and high position power.

3. *Low control* situations offer the leader relatively low control and influence, that is, where the group does not support the leader, and neither the task nor his position power give him much influence. Stress or high group conflict may also contribute to low control.

Third, there are three dimensions that determine the situational control of a job. These are:

1. Leader-member relations measures how well the group and the leader get along.

2. Task structure measures how clearly the procedures, goals, and evaluation of the job are defined.

3. Position power measures how much authority to hire and fire and discipline the leader has.

Fourth, in matching leadership styles to appropriate situations we find that:

1. *Relationship-motivated* leaders perform best in moderate control situations.

2. *Task-motivated* leaders perform best in high and low control situations.

Finally, it is possible to change or modify your leadership situation if you find that your leadership style does not match the situation in which you are working. You can engineer your job by adjusting the three dimensions of situational control and making it higher or lower, thereby matching your leadership style. Transfer and rotation, selection and placement, are management tools to improve the performance of your subordinate leaders, thereby increasing organizational effectiveness.

Suggested Readings

Chemers, M.M. and Skrzypek, G.J. An experimental test of the Contingency Model of Leadership Effectiveness. *Journal of Personality and Social Psychology* 1972, 24:172-177.

Chemers, M.M., Rice, R.W., Sundstrom, E., and Butler, W.M. Leader esteem for the least preferred co-worker score, training, and effectiveness: An experimental examination. *Journal of Personality and Social Psychology* 1975, 31:401-409.

Fiedler, F.E. Engineer the job to fit the manager. *Harvard Business Review* 1965, 43:116-112.

Fiedler, F.E. *A theory of leadership effectiveness.* New York: McGraw-Hill, 1967.

Fiedler, F.E. Style or circumstance: The leadership enigma. *Psychology Today* 1969.

Fiedler, F.E. Leadership experience and leader performance — Another hypothesis shot to hell. *Organizational Behavior and Human Performance* 1970, 5:1-14.

Fiedler, F.E. Validation and extension of the Contingency Model of leadership effectiveness: A review of empirical findings. *Psychological Bulletin* 1971, 76:128-148.

Fiedler, F.E. *Leadership.* New York: General Learning Press, 1971.

Fiedler, F.E. How do you make leaders more effective? New answers to an old puzzle. *Organizational Dynamics* 1972, 1:3-18.

Fiedler, F.E. The effects of leadership training and experience: A Contingency Model interpretation. *Administrative Science Quarterly* 1972, 17:453-470.

Fiedler, F.E. Stimulus/Response: The trouble with leadership training is that it doesn't train leaders. *Psychology Today* 1973, 6:23-92.

Fiedler, F.E. The Contingency Model — New directions for leadership utilization. *Contemporary Business* 1974, 65-79.

Fiedler, F.E. and Chemers, M.M. *Leadership and effective management.* New York: Scott Foresman, 1974.

Fiedler, F.E. The Leadership Game: Matching the man to the situation. *Organizational Dynamics* 1976, Winter: 6-16.

Index

Leader Match Scales

This Appendix includes a copy of each of the scales needed to apply the concepts of Leader Match. These scales, on perforated pages which may be easily torn out, should serve as master copies to be reproduced as needed.

LEADER-MEMBER RELATIONS SCALE

Circle the number which best represents your response to each item.

	strongly agree	agree	neither agree nor disagree	disagree	strongly disagree
1. The people I supervise have trouble getting along with each other.	1	2	3	4	5
2. My subordinates are reliable and trustworthy.	5	4	3	2	1
3. There seems to be a friendly atmosphere among the people I supervise.	5	4	3	2	1
4. My subordinates always cooperate with me in getting the job done.	5	4	3	2	1
5. There is friction between my subordinates and myself.	1	2	3	4	5
6. My subordinates give me a good deal of help and support in getting the job done.	5	4	3	2	1
7. The people I supervise work well together in getting the job done.	5	4	3	2	1
8. I have good relations with the people I supervise.	5	4	3	2	1

Total Score [ ]

TASK STRUCTURE RATING SCALE — PART I

Circle the number in the appropriate column.	Usually True	Sometimes True	Seldom True
Is the Goal Clearly Stated or Known?			
1. Is there a blueprint, picture, model or detailed description available of the finished product or service?	2	1	0
2. Is there a person available to advise and give a description of the finished product or service, or how the job should be done?	2	1	0
Is There Only One Way to Accomplish the Task?			
3. Is there a step-by-step procedure, or a standard operating procedure which indicates in detail the process which is to be followed?	2	1	0
4. Is there a specific way to subdivide the task into separate parts or steps?	2	1	0
5. Are there some ways which are clearly recognized as better than others for performing this task?	2	1	0
Is There Only One Correct Answer or Solution?			
6. Is it obvious when the task is finished and the correct solution has been found?	2	1	0
7. Is there a book, manual, or job description which indicates the best solution or the best outcome for the task?	2	1	0
Is It Easy to Check Whether the Job Was Done Right?			
8. Is there a generally agreed understanding about the standards the particular product or service has to meet to be considered acceptable?	2	1	0
9. Is the evaluation of this task generally made on some quantitative basis?	2	1	0
10. Can the leader and the group find out how well the task has been accomplished in enough time to improve future performance?	2	1	0

SUBTOTAL ☐

TASK STRUCTURE RATING SCALE — PART 2

Training and Experience Adjustment

NOTE: Do not adjust jobs with task structure scores of 6 or below.

(a) Compared to others in this or similar positions, how much *training* has the leader had?

3	2	1	0
No training at all	Very little training	A moderate amount of training	A great deal of training

(b) Compared to others in this or similar positions, how much *experience* has the leader had?

6	4	2	0
No experience at all	Very little experience	A moderate amount of experience	A great deal of experience

Add lines (a) and (b) of the training and experience adjustment, then *subtract* this from the subtotal given in Part 1.

Subtotal from Part 1.

Subtract training and experience adjustment

Total Task Structure Score

POSITION POWER RATING SCALE

Circle the number which best represents your answer.

1. Can the leader directly or by recommendation administer rewards and punishments to his subordinates?

2	1	0
Can act directly or can recommend with high effectiveness	Can recommend but with mixed results	No

2. Can the leader directly or by recommendation affect the promotion, demotion, hiring or firing of his subordinates?

2	1	0
Can act directly or can recommend with high effectiveness	Can recommend but with mixed results	No

3. Does the leader have the knowledge necessary to assign tasks to subordinates and instruct them in task completion?

2	1	0
Yes	Sometimes or in some aspects	No

4. Is it the leader's job to evaluate the performance of his subordinates?

2	1	0
Yes	Sometimes or in some aspects	No

5. Has the leader been given some official title of authority by the organization (e.g., foreman, department head, platoon leader)?

2	0
Yes	No

Total

SITUATIONAL CONTROL SCALE

Enter the total scores for the Leader-Member Relations dimension, the Task Structure scale, and the Position Power scale in the spaces below. Add the three scores together and compare your total with the ranges given in the table below to determine your overall situational control.

1. *Leader-Member Relations Total*

2. *Task Structure Total*

3. *Position Power Total*

Grand Total

Total Score	51 - 70	31 - 50	10 - 30
Amount of Situational Control	High Control	Moderate Control	Low Control